320.9
GOV

3 6480 000070260   ☑ W9-BML-715

RECEIVED

AUG 2 2 2000

NJ Dept. of Labor Library
Trenton, NJ   08625-0943

Government to Government

Understanding
State and Tribal Governments

By
Susan Johnson
Jeanne Kaufmann
National Conference of State Legislatures

John Dossett
Sarah Hicks
National Congress of American Indians

NATIONAL CONFERENCE
of STATE LEGISLATURES

William T. Pound, Executive Director

1560 Broadway, Suite 700
Denver, Colorado 80202
(303) 830-2200

444 North Capitol Street, N.W.
Washington, D.C. 20001
(202) 624-5400

NATIONAL CONGRESS
OF AMERICAN INDIANS

JoAnn Chase, Executive Director

1301 Connecticut Ave., N.W.
Suite 200
Washington, D.C. 20036
(202) 466-7767

June 2000

The National Conference of State Legislatures (NCSL) serves the legislators and staffs of the nation's 50 states, its commonwealths, and territories. NCSL is a bipartisan organization with three objectives:

- To improve the quality and effectiveness of state legislatures,
- To foster interstate communication and cooperation,
- To ensure states a strong cohesive voice in the federal system.

The Conference operates from offices in Denver, Colorado, and Washington, D.C.

The National Congress of American Indians (NCAI) was founded in 1944 in response to termination and assimilation policies that the United States forced upon tribal governments in contradiction of their treaty rights and status as sovereigns. NCAI stressed the need for unity and cooperation among native governments for the protection of their treaty and sovereign rights. Since 1944, the National Congress of American Indians has been working to inform the public and Congress on the governmental rights of American Indians and Alaska Natives.

Now as in the past, NCAI serves to:

- Secure to ourselves and our descendants the rights and benefits to which we are entitled,
- Enlighten the public toward the better understanding of the Indian people,
- Preserve rights under Indian treaties or agreements with the United States, and
- Promote the common welfare of the American Indians and Alaska Natives.

Printed on recycled paper

©2000 by the National Conference of State Legislatures. All rights reserved.
ISBN 1-58024-110-7

CONTENTS

PREFACE AND ACKNOWLEDGMENTS

A joint project between the National Conference of State Legislatures (NCSL) and the National Congress of American Indians (NCAI) attempts to promote intergovernmental cooperation between states and tribes by researching, assessing and disseminating information about how devolution will affect Indian tribes and the state-tribal relationship.

States and tribes have mutual interests: to use public resources effectively and efficiently, to provide comprehensive services to their respective citizens, to protect the natural environment, and to sustain economies. These mutual interests have, at times, created jurisdictional disputes that historically have been solved through litigation. The purpose of this project, however, is to facilitate state-tribal cooperation.

State legislators and tribal leaders have not been previously provided with a consistent neutral forum to address these issues. Providers of information to both state and tribal leaders generally may be biased or suspect for a variety of reasons. State and tribal leaders may not feel entirely comfortable dealing with one another due to lack of cultural or procedural (e.g., the state legislative process) understanding. In addition, state and tribal leaders may not realize that cooperative measures are possible to deal with many mutual issues.

Based on recognizing mutual needs and increasing causes for intergovernmental relations between states and tribes highlighted by devolution, overarching goals of this project include the following:

- Promote an understanding of tribal sovereignty and governance by state legislators, and promote an understanding among tribal leaders regarding issues and processes of state governance, in an attempt to alleviate some of the basic and historical mistrust that tribes may feel toward states.
- Create and maintain neutral forums that are comfortable for and conducive to fostering improved state-tribal leader relationships.
- Understand how to form effective state-tribal agreements to meet mutual interests (what works, what doesn't).
- Create and institutionalize resource networks.

This publication provides information for state legislators about tribal governments and for tribal leaders about state governments. Primary barriers to good relations are lack of knowledge and misunderstandings, resulting in an inability for tribal and state governments to simply relate to one another.

Much, if not all, of this information is published in various formats. It is gathered in this publication to assist tribal and state elected officials who have many concurrent issues and limited time to address them—to provide some basic information that officials of both states and tribes often lack about one another.

Although this guide does not provide comprehensive information about existing models of state-tribal cooperation, it does include a chapter about why working with neighboring governments is important for both governments.

An advisory council to this project provided conceptual support and editorial comments on drafts of this document. We would like to thank the following advisory council members:

Chairman W. Ron Allen
  Jamestown S'Klallam
  Tribal Council

Senator Dennis Bercier
  North Dakota

President Robert Chicks
  Stockbridge-Munsee
  Community of Wisconsin

Senator Kelly Haney
  Oklahoma

LaDonna Harris, President
  Americans for Indian
  Opportunity

President Audrey Kohnen
  Prairie Island Indian
  Community of Minnesota

David Lovell, Senior Analyst
  Wisconsin Legislative
  Council Staff

Senator Lana Oleen
  Kansas

Senator Margarita Prentice
  Washington

Senator Tim Sheldon
  Washington

Melvin Sheldon
  Council Member
  Tulalip Tribe

Gail Small, Director
  Native Action

Thanks to Karen Quigley, executive director of the Oregon Legislative Commission on Indian Services; NCSL Legislative Management Program Director Brian Weberg and staff Tim Storey; Dr. Eddie F. Brown, associate dean, George Warren Brown School of Social Work; Cyndi Holmes, self governance director, Jamestown S'Klallam Tribe; and Heather Wood, NCAI staff assistant for reviewing drafts of this document; NCSL editorial staff Leann Stelzer and Scott Liddell for editing and formatting; and NCSL Publications Director Karen Hansen and Executive Director Bill Pound for their understanding. Thanks also to Sam Deloria and the American Indian Law Center for the years of work in tribal-state relations and all the information he provided to us.

Finally, special thanks to the W.K. Kellogg Foundation, for realizing the importance of and funding this effort.

ABOUT THE AUTHORS

This guidebook was produced jointly by the National Conference of State Legislatures (NCSL) and the National Congress of American Indians (NCAI).

At NCSL, Susan Johnson is the project manager and Jeanne Kaufmann is a research analyst for the state-tribal relations project.

At NCAI, John Dossett and Sarah Hicks are co-managers, and Andrea Howard is a research analyst for the state-tribal relations project.

Executive Summary

State and tribal governments have common purposes: to use public resources effectively and efficiently, to provide comprehensive services to their respective citizens, and to protect the natural environment, all while sustaining healthy economies. Neighboring governments, as a practical matter, share many aspects of their respective economic and social systems, and are connected through political and legal relationships. Although these mutual interests have created jurisdictional disputes that historically have been solved through litigation, there is an increasing need for cooperation. Public resources are an issue for all governments, and states and tribes can benefit by collaborating and pooling resources to the fullest extent possible.

As tribal governments continue to build their capabilities and exercise their powers of self-government, and as the federal government continues to devolve responsibilities to them, states and tribes must address policy questions that concern jurisdiction and shared governance. Tribal and state governments exercise many of the same sovereign powers: taxing, licensing and regulation, and making and enforcing laws. States and tribes also are responsible for governmental services such as education, environmental protection and basic infrastructure.

Tribal and state governments exercise many of the same sovereign powers.

State-tribal relations have focused primarily on executive branches in the states through issue-specific relations with particular agencies and, increasingly, on a broader scale through commissions and government-to-government agreements with

State legislatures can be a powerful forum in which to deal with state-tribal relations.

governors. However, state legislatures can be a powerful forum in which to deal with state-tribal relations, because they have the primary responsibility to develop state policies governing resource allocations and give authority and direction to agencies to carry out programs and provide services.

If legislators are uninformed or misinformed about the unique circumstances and needs of Indian communities, those tribal citizens will not be adequately served. If tribal governments do not understand state governance concerns and positions, or do not believe that working with states can be beneficial, then opportunities for cooperation will not be realized. State and tribal leaders may not feel entirely comfortable or confident dealing with one another because of past history or lack of understanding of the other. If the tribes and states are to work together successfully, they will want to overcome these problems of trust and other barriers. An understanding of government structures and procedures—as well as cultural issues—is necessary for both tribes and states.

1. Introduction

Indian Nations and States: Sovereign Governments, Mutual Interests and Common Concerns

The U.S. Constitution recognizes Indian nations as governments, and hundreds of treaties, federal laws and court cases have repeatedly affirmed that American Indian nations retain the inherent powers to govern themselves. The concept of state sovereignty arises from the Constitution's Tenth Amendment, which states: "The powers not delegated to the United States by the Constitution, nor prohibited by it to the States, are reserved to the States respectively, or to the people."

State governments and tribal governments have far more in common than they have in conflict. Both types of government have a primary interest in protecting the health and welfare of their people. Both want to promote the economy, provide jobs, protect natural resources and the environment, and provide governmental services. Both tribes and states have to balance these issues, and their budgets, in order to meet the needs and demands of their constituents. The ongoing devolution of federal programs to the state and tribal levels also has increased the number of common concerns that states and tribes have.

State governments and tribal governments have far more in common than they have in conflict.

Interactions Between States and Tribes Are Changing

Across the 35 states where there are many federally recognized tribes, tribal governments are increasing their capabilities and exercising their powers of self-government on matters ranging from natural resource management to economic development to social services programs to judicial responsibilities. These activities sometimes generate friction with state governments, but more often bring new opportunities for cooperation and mutually beneficial relations. Some states have encountered legal difficulties when dealing with tribes, but other states can provide examples of cooperative agreements and enabling legislation for negotiation processes, commissions, committees and special activities.

In recent years, more state legislatures have established forums—separate from those of the executive branches—to address Indian affairs. Some states have hybrid commissions or committees (see appendix A). Regardless of what forum exists, there are some common sense reasons why state legislators and tribal leaders may want or need to work together.

Cooperation and Mutual Respect Leads to Positive Results for Both Tribes and States

Tribal governments, state governments and local governments are finding innovative ways to work together to carry out their governmental functions.

Many tribes and states are discovering ways to set aside jurisdictional debate in favor of cooperative government-to-government relationships that respect the autonomy of both governments. Tribal governments, state governments and local governments are finding innovative ways to work together to carry out their governmental functions. New intergovernmental institutions have been developed in many states, and state-tribal cooperative agreements on a broad range of issues are becoming commonplace.

Cooperative Agreements Protect Jurisdiction and Avoid Expensive Legal Conflicts

Cooperation does not mean that either a state or a tribe is giving away jurisdiction or sovereignty. Some areas of disagreement may always exist, as they may with any neighboring governments. Certainly, both states and tribes will preserve their ability to litigate over jurisdictional, legal and constitutional rights when it is in their best interest to do so. However, many costly and unproductive legal conflicts can be avoided and many beneficial results can be obtained through efforts by both states and tribes to understand each other and resolve conflicts. This guide is intended to help states and tribes understand each other and begin the process of exploring new avenues for improvement of governmental service for the citizens of both tribes and states.

Because devolution may result in overlapping or parallel responsibilities for state and tribal governments, there is mutual interest in coordinating services and authorities to eliminate duplication and to maximize limited resources. State and tribal governments can establish lines of communication, and can work toward coordinated governing. Devolution, in giving greater responsibility to state and tribal governments, not only has increased opportunities for conflict but also has increased opportunities for meaningful and mutually beneficial cooperation.

Devolution has increased opportunities for meaningful and mutually beneficial cooperation.

Devolution
A major impetus for the increased need for improved tribal-state relations is devolution—the transfer of resources and responsibilities, often through federal block grants or other funding mechanisms, to state, local or tribal governments. This shifting of power and authority away from the federal government is intended to "bring government closer to the people," and make government more responsive to local needs. Response to local needs is much more difficult to accomplish through a large federal bureaucracy. In recent years, service

programs (welfare reform, child care, social support) and environmental programs have been increasingly devolved from the federal government to states and tribes.

Devolution's Effect on Tribal Governments

Devolution disproportionately affects tribal governments. Depending on the mechanism through which programs are devolved (generally through federal law), tribal governments may or may not be recognized as units of government with authority to directly receive the resources and administer the specific program. Although some authorizing laws—like many environmental laws and the welfare reform law—recognize tribal governments as capable program administrators, other federal laws do not. For instance, sections of the Social Security Act authorize only state governments to administer Medicaid, Medicare and Children's Health Insurance Programs. Even when tribes are authorized to administer programs similar to state programs, tribes often are afforded proportionally fewer resources and subjected to greater oversight than are states. Federal devolutionary policies are inconsistent in regard to the sovereign status of tribal governments and their capacity to carry out governmental programs.

Federal devolutionary policies are inconsistent in regard to the sovereign status of tribal governments and their capacity to carry out governmental programs.

Before or in the early stages of the current devolutionary trend, many tribal governments and the federal government embraced the concept of shifting federal programs and services to tribal control. The Indian Self-Determination and Education Assistance Act of 1975 gave Indian tribes the authority to contract for federal resources and administer federal programs as a basic exercise of tribal sovereignty and self-determination. Since 1975, the self-determination programs have been expanded several times, and the Self-Governance Act of 1994 gave tribes even greater flexibility in reprogramming Bureau of Indian Affairs and Indian Health Services resources to meet tribal needs. The premise of the self-determination and self-governance programs is that tribal governments have the option to negotiate an agreement to receive the federal resources and perform the services themselves. This ability of each tribe to negotiate an arrangement that will meet its unique needs is key to the success of the self-determination and self-governance programs; it is lacking in other forms of federal devolution.

Devolutionary policies also raise questions about whether devolution will diminish the federal trust responsibility to tribes and reduce federal oversight and concern for tribal needs. The trust responsibility is the obligation of the federal government to protect tribal self-governance, tribal lands, assets, resources, and treaty rights, and generally to ensure that the basic needs of tribal communities are met (discussed in more detail in chapter 2). The self-determination and self-governance acts clearly guard the federal trust responsibility, but other forms of federal devolution do not. Because of the inconsistent history of federal Indian policy, tribes are hesitant to rely upon policies that attempt to make them self-sufficient. Such polices often have been accompanied by efforts to remove the federal protection of tribal self-government and the federal responsibility for tribal needs.

So, while tribal governments generally welcome the opportunity for increased authority and flexibility, they also question the long-term effects of devolutionary policies and their differential acknowledgment of tribal governments. As a result, tribal acceptance of devolved programs has varied greatly. Tribes generally desire that both the federal and the state governments give greater consideration to tribal self-government and unique tribal needs as devolved programs are developed and implemented.

Common Concerns

In spite of some disparate treatment, state and tribal governments have many similar interests in devolutionary policies. Both states and tribes have wrestled with the new responsibilities and federal limitations, and have consistently sought greater flexibility. Tribes and states have a great interest in collaborating to ensure that services are efficiently provided to all citizens—both inside and outside reservation boundaries—and in minimizing service overlap.

Both states and tribes have wrestled with new responsibilities and federal limitations and have consistently sought greater flexibility.

*Some devolved
programs have
limited program and
policy development
flexibility.*

State and tribal governments similarly struggle to have an opportunity to provide input into congressional processes that develop the structure and limitations with which programs are devolved. Adequate resources to provide services also are of concern, particularly because fixed federal block grants may be inadequate in times of economic distress or downturn. Finally, some devolved programs have limited program and policy development flexibility, unrealistic programmatic performance measures, lack administrative resources and have overburdensome reporting requirements, all which are problematic for both states and tribes. In the era of devolution, state and tribal governments have many common interests and communication and collaboration are increasingly necessary.

2. STRUCTURE AND OPERATION OF TRIBAL GOVERNMENTS

More than 558 federally recognized "Indian tribes" (variously called tribes, nations, bands, pueblos, communities and native villages) exist in the United States. About 226 of these are located in Alaska; the rest are located in 34 other states. Tribes are ethnically, culturally and linguistically diverse.

Article 1, Section 8 of the U.S. Constitution reads, "The Congress shall have power to...regulate commerce with foreign nations, and among the several states, and with the Indian tribes." Thus, the supreme law of the United States clearly recognizes the governmental status of Indian tribes and creates the basis for the unique federal relationship with tribal governments. The Supreme Court, the president and the Congress have repeatedly affirmed that Indian tribes retain their inherent powers of self-government.

The Supreme Court, the president and the Congress have repeatedly affirmed that Indian tribes retain their inherent powers of self-government.

To understand today's tribal governments, it is helpful to know the basic history of federal policy toward Indian tribes.

Federal Policy Toward Indian Nations

Pre-1492 *Pre-Columbian Period*—Indian people lived in organized societies with their own forms of government for thousands of years before contact with Europeans.

1492-1828 *Colonial Period*—The proliferation of European colonies created a dominant presence on the East Coast of North America. These colonies acquired some Indian lands under the doctrine of discovery and also signed treaties with the tribes for additional land. Colonial governments treated with Indian tribes as governments, setting the precedent for future relations. Following the Revolutionary War, the newborn United States took pains to maintain peace with neighboring tribes, but pressure from settlers resulted in increasing encroachment and conflict.

Colonial governments treated with Indian tribes as governments, setting the precedent for future relations.

1828-1887 *Removal, Reservation and Treaty Period*—As the U.S. population and military strength grew, so did pressure by the U.S. government on eastern tribes to move west, resulting in forced migration and the creation of treaty reservations. Later, the U.S. government embarked on an aggressive military policy throughout the West and established Indian reservations through treaties, acquiring more Indian land. In general, the treaties traded land for the right to tribal self-governance on reservations under the protection of the United States.

1887-1934 *Allotment and Assimilation Period*—Settlers' increasing desire for the land within reservations and the push to assimilate Indians into mainstream American life led to the General Allotment Act of 1887 (also known as the Dawes Act), which dictated the forced conversion of communally held tribal lands into small parcels for individual Indian ownership. More than 90 million acres— nearly two-thirds of reservation land—were taken from tribes and given to settlers, most often without compensation to the tribes.

1934-1945 *Indian Reorganization Period*—The federal government, under the Indian Reorganization Act of 1934, was prevented from carrying out further allotment. It began to restore Indian lands to tribes and attempted to help tribes reform their governments. The federal government created programs and projects to rehabilitate Indian economic life. These efforts were critical in reestablishing tribal economies and formed a basis for renewed tribal autonomy, but too often forced European/Anglo values and government structures upon tribes, thereby damaging traditional values and governance.

1945-1968 *Termination Period*—Congress decided that federal assistance to more than 100 tribes should be terminated. Public Law 280, passed in 1953, imposed state criminal and civil jurisdiction on many tribes in California, Minnesota, Nebraska, Oregon and Wisconsin. These policies created economic disaster for many tribes, and millions of acres of valuable natural resource land were removed through tax forfeiture sales. Federal policy emphasized the physical relocation of Indians from reservations to urban areas.

1968-present *Self-Determination Period*—A resurgence of tribal government activity in Congress and in the federal courts ended the termination era and pushed U.S. policy toward self-determination and self-governance. Policies emerged that favored tribal control over their destinies. With control over their lands and resources, tribes have made great strides toward reversing the economic blight that resulted from previous federal policies, and have revived their unique cultures and societies. Under the self-determination and self-governance acts, tribal governments have been managing many federal programs that are intended to serve Indian people.

Tribal Sovereignty

The essence of tribal sovereignty is the ability to govern and to protect the health, safety and welfare of tribal citizens within tribal territory. Tribes are separate and distinct peoples with unique histories that predate the United States as a political entity. Recognition of and respect for tribal sovereignty has strong roots that date to the earliest contact between the indigenous peoples of North America and the first European

The essence of tribal sovereignty is the ability to govern and to protect the health, safety and welfare of tribal citizens within tribal territory.

settlers. Settlers and the tribal leaders dealt with each other as separate sovereigns, and that relationship is the foundation of all interactions that have taken place between the United States and Indian tribes throughout the history of the nation. This policy of respect for tribal sovereignty is found in the U.S. Constitution, nation-to-nation treaties, federal statutes, case law, executive orders and other administrative policies.

Just as the United States deals with states as governments, it also deals with Indian tribes as governments, not as special interest groups, individuals or some other type of non-governmental entity. Many state governments also have explicitly recognized the governmental status of Indian tribes through various state recognition processes.

Tribal governments have the inherent right to develop their own form of government, to determine their own citizenship, to establish their own civil and criminal laws and be ruled by them in tribal courts, to tax, to license and regulate, and to exclude people from tribal lands. Tribal governments are responsible for a broad range of governmental activities on tribal lands, including education; law enforcement; justice systems; environmental protection; and basic infrastructure such as roads, bridges, sewers, solid waste treatment and disposal, and public buildings.

Congress and the federal courts have placed some significant limitations on the exercise of tribal sovereignty, particularly with regard to jurisdiction over non-Indians. For example, tribal jurisdiction over non-Indians on criminal matters was sharply limited in the 1978 Supreme Court decision in *Oliphant vs. Suquamish Indian Tribe.* However, federal law is particularly protective of tribes' authority over internal matters and their ability to protect the health and welfare of their people. Tribal sovereignty is inherent in the status of Indian tribes, and the law assumes that tribes have sovereign authority unless a federal statute has specifically removed that authority or a federal court has determined that the tribe's exer-

Federal law is particularly protective of tribes' authority over internal matters

cise of authority is completely inconsistent with the tribal status within the federal framework.

The status of Indian nations as governments and the preservation and protection of tribal history, language, culture and traditions are at the heart of almost every issue that touches Indian Country and often are misunderstood or not considered by non-Indians. Self-government is essential for tribal communities to continue to protect their unique cultures and identities, and tribal cultures and traditions provide the foundation upon which Indian communities are governed.

Relationship to State Sovereignty

The Constitution gives authority in Indian affairs to the federal government, not to the state governments. Tribal governments are not subservient to state governments, and retain the right to create laws that are stricter or more lenient than state laws. State laws cannot be applied where they interfere with the right of a tribe to make its own laws protecting the health and welfare of its citizens, or where it would interfere with any federal interest. In general, states may regulate only on matters that are exclusive to non-Indians and that do not affect tribal interests. In some limited instances, the federal government has delegated federal authority on Indian lands to the states.

The analysis of state-tribal relations often is described as a jurisdictional battle over when and how the state may regulate on tribal lands. However, this view of tribal-state relations is incomplete. With far less publicity, tribal governments and state governments for many decades have found ways to cooperate on a broad range of regulatory matters. Most often, the cooperation is in the form of an intergovernmental agreement, a state statute, or an informal arrangement regarding which government will cover certain functions.

Tribal governments and state governments for many decades have found ways to cooperate on a broad range of regulatory matters.

Treaties

When European settlers came to America, they dealt with the tribes as sovereigns and often negotiated treaties. Exchanges of land and guarantees of peace were handled by treaty. The U.S. government continued to deal with the tribes through treaties until after the Revolutionary War.

Hundreds of treaties have been negotiated between Indian nations and the United States.

Hundreds of treaties between Indian nations and the United States have been negotiated by the president and ratified by two-thirds of the Senate. Indian treaties have the same status as treaties with foreign nations. Because such treaties are made under the U.S. Constitution, they take precedence over any conflicting state law. Terms of the treaties are upheld by the Supreme Court, although the Court has ruled that treaties may be unilaterally abrogated by Congress. However, Congress must show a "clear and plain" intent to abrogate a treaty (*Lone Wolf vs. Hitchcock, 1903*).

Treaties vary widely in their terms and provisions. They commonly included a guarantee of peace, a provision on land boundaries, a guarantee of hunting and fishing rights (often on lands outside the reservation lands) and a statement that the tribe recognized the authority of the United States and, in return, received a promise from the United States of protection.

Indian treaty making effectively ended in 1871 when Congress passed a legislative rider that attempted to limit the power of the president to enter into treaties with Indian nations. Although some question the constitutionality of this legislation, it nevertheless made clear that no further treaties would be ratified. As a result, not all tribes have a treaty. Although the U.S. Senate did ratify 370 Indian treaties between 1778 and 1871, at least another 45 were negotiated with tribes but never ratified. As determined by the U.S. Court of Claims, some of these unratified treaties have taken legal effect. After official treaty making ended, many tribes have been federally recognized through executive order or statute.

Trust Relationship

The federal trust responsibility, one of the most important doctrines in federal Indian law, derives from the treaties and the European law of nations. It is the obligation of the federal government to protect tribal self-governance, tribal lands, assets, resources, and treaty rights, and to carry out the directions of federal statutes and court cases. The Supreme Court has defined the trust responsibility as "moral obligations of the highest responsibility and trust" (*Seminole Nation vs. United States, 1942*).

The federal trust responsibility is the obligation of the federal government to protect tribal self-governance, tribal lands, assets, resources, and treaty rights.

The trust responsibility can be broadly divided into two interrelated areas. The property-oriented trust duties concentrate upon a narrow but important aspect of the federal trust responsibility: protecting tribal property and assets where the title is held in trust by the United States for the benefit of the tribe. The second, more fundamental, federal trust obligation is to honor the federal guarantee of self-government and the promise that tribal lands must be preserved as the base for a separate culture. A permanent tribal community requires a secure land base to function upon and govern, water to irrigate the land, fish and game in the streams, and income from timber and mineral development. The federal trustee is under an obligation to protect those purposes.

The trust responsibility has also been acknowledged in the Snyder Act of 1921, which requires that the Bureau of Indian Affairs, under the supervision of the secretary of the Interior Department, "to direct, supervise, and expend such moneys as Congress may from time to time appropriate, for the benefit, care and assistance of Indians throughout the United States" for several purposes, including education; health; economic development and profitability of Indian property; development and maintenance of Indian water supplies and buildings; the hiring of government officials, physicians, Indian police, and Indian judges; and the suppression of drug and alcohol trafficking.

The Structure of Tribal Governments

The 558 federally recognized tribes in the United States today have governments that are diverse in structure and in decision-making processes.

Traditional tribal governments existed long before European contact and have evolved over time. The 558 federally recognized tribes in the United States today have governments that are diverse in structure and in decision-making processes. Because some tribal constitutions were patterned after the model constitution developed by the Bureau of Indian Affairs—in response to the Indian Reorganization Act (IRA) of 1934— some similarities exist among tribal governments. These standard tribal constitutions contain provisions describing tribal territory, specifying eligibility for citizenship, and establishing the governing bodies and their powers.

Most tribes give legislative authority to a tribal council. In some tribes, the tribal council members are elected by district; in others, they are elected at large. The council generally has authority to write tribal laws, and in some tribes the council members have administrative duties. Most tribal constitutions also provide for an executive officer, called a tribal chairman, president, governor or chief. In some tribes, the chief executive is elected by the tribal council, while in others he or she is directly elected by the voting citizens. In most cases, the duties and powers of the chief executive are not specified in the constitution, but are set in the bylaws. Consequently, the role of the chief executive varies greatly among tribes. Many tribes also have created their own court systems that administer codes passed by the tribal council. In many tribes, judges are elected by popular vote; in others, judges are appointed by the tribal council.

About 60 percent of tribal governments are based on Indian Reorganization Act constitutions. Tribes that have chosen other structures and constitutions frequently have made the decision to do so in favor of a government that is more traditional to the tribe, and do not necessarily follow the pattern outlined above. Such governments are diverse and range from the Navajo Nation to the pueblos of New Mexico. The Navajo Nation has no written constitution, but operates under a detailed tribal code and has an elected council and president. Many of the pueblos operate entirely under unwritten customary law, with traditional leadership and a completely different government structure.

Tribal Lands

Land is of great spiritual and cultural significance to Indian tribes, and many Indian communities continue to rely upon the land for subsistence through hunting, fishing and gathering. Land-based production such as agriculture, forestry, mining, and oil and gas production play a prominent role in tribal economies. Moreover, Indian lands are critical for the exercise of tribal self-governance and self-determination.

Between 1887 and 1934, the U.S. government took more than 90 million acres—nearly two-thirds of reservation lands—from the tribes and gave it to settlers, most often without compensation to the tribes. In addition, the termination era of the 1940s and 1950s resulted in the loss of huge amounts of reservation land.

Today, Indian tribes hold more than 50 million acres of land, approximately 2 percent of the United States. Most of these lands are in arid and remote regions. The largest reservation— the Navajo Nation—covers an area as large as West Virginia. Some reservations are as small as a few acres, and some tribes hold no land at all. With the exception of Metlakatla in Southeast Alaska, no reservations exist in that state. Alaska Native lands title is outlined in the Alaska Native Settlement Claims Act of 1971.

Trust Lands

Title to most tribal lands is held by the federal government in trust for the benefit of current and future generations of tribal citizens. Most often, this land is within the boundaries of a reservation. Although trust land falls under tribal government authority and generally is not subject to state laws, it also is

Title to most tribal lands is held by the federal government in trust.

subject to limitations on the use of the land and requires federal approval for most actions. As a result of allotment, a great deal of land is held in trust status for individuals.

Trust status can be conferred only by the secretary of interior or the U.S. Congress by statute.

Under the 1934 Indian Reorganization Act, the federal government and the tribes can acquire additional land in trust in an effort to "... conserve and develop Indian lands and resources" and to rehabilitate Indian economic life. This land usually is purchased by the tribe or acquired from federal surplus lands. Trust status can be conferred only by the secretary of interior or the U.S. Congress by statute.

Since 1934, the secretary has taken about 9 million acres back into trust status—about 10 percent of the total amount of land lost. The vast majority of reacquired lands have been within the boundaries of existing reservations. However, it is sometimes necessary for tribes to acquire land outside reservation boundaries. This is particularly true for tribes that have extremely small reservations, for those in remote areas far from the mainstream of economic life, and for those tribes where reservations were diminished during the allotment or termination periods.

Regulations require that the secretary notify state and local governments before making a determination on taking land into trust status, and the secretary must specifically consider the effect on state and local governments of removal of the land from the tax rolls. State and local governments have the right to appeal a secretarial decision both within the Department of Interior and in the federal courts.

Much stricter limitations exist on acquiring land into trust if that land is to be used by a tribal government for gaming purposes. The Indian Gaming Regulatory Act of 1988 (25 U.S.C. §2719) prohibits gaming on off-reservation lands that were acquired in trust after 1988, unless the governor of the state concurs and the secretary determines that gaming would not be detrimental to the surrounding community.

Non-Indian Fee Lands

One of the chief issues regarding Indian lands is the effect of former federal land policies—including allotment—that left many tribes with scattered and fractionated parcels intermixed with lands held by non-Indians. This landholding pattern, often called "checkerboarding," creates two primary problems. The first is that it may render the tribal land base unusable for agriculture, grazing, timber or mining.

The second problem that arises is the jurisdiction over non-Indian fee land within reservation boundaries. Some non-Indians do not want a tribal government to have jurisdiction over their land, and tribal governments resent the intrusion of state jurisdiction within tribal boundaries. In general, the Supreme Court has confirmed the authority of tribal governments to exercise civil authority over the conduct of non-Indians on fee lands within a reservation when that conduct threatens the political integrity, the economic security, or the health and welfare of the tribe *(Montana vs. U.S., 1981)*. In practice, jurisdictional matters on checkerboard lands offer a prime opportunity for increased coordination and the development of cooperative agreements between tribal, state and local officials.

Jurisdictional matters on checkerboard lands offer a prime opportunity for increased coordination between tribal, state and local officials.

Answers to Frequently Asked Questions About Indian Nations

Why are Indian tribal citizens treated differently than racial minority groups such as African Americans, Latinos, Asian Americans and others?

American Indians and Alaska Natives are members or citizens of tribal governments. The tribal government has a special legal and political relationship with the federal government, and certain services are provided by the U.S. government because the person is a citizen of the tribe. American Indians and Alaska Natives also are citizens of the United States and their states, with rights to vote and run for office.

What are the requirements for tribal citizenship?

Like any government, tribal governments determine their own criteria for citizenship. Usually there is some blood quantum requirement, such as 1/4, or a requirement of lineal descendance from a tribal citizen. Individual tribes can answer specific questions. Some federal agencies also have criteria for determining eligibility for programs and services. About 2.3 million Native people in the United States are enrolled citizens of federally recognized tribes.

American Indians and Alaska Natives are citizens of the United States and their states, with rights to vote and run for office.

Does the federal government provide all the necessary funding for Indian tribes?

Like state governments, tribal governments receive some federal funding for the programs they operate. The federal government has an obligation to tribal governments that is based on numerous treaties and on the overall trust responsibility. Despite these obligations, federal funding is inadequate as are the services and infrastructure of many tribal governments on Indian reservations.

Does the federal government pay all expenses—health care, housing and college tuition—for individual Indians?

In general, no. The federal government provides basic health care for all Indian people through the Indian Health Service. Unfortunately, these health programs have been inadequately funded for many decades, and Indian people have the worst health status of any group in the country. The Department of Housing and Urban Services provides some housing on Indian reservations, but Indians have the highest rate of homelessness and overcrowding. The federal government provides some educational assistance to tribal colleges, but higher education generally is not provided and remains beyond the reach of most Indian people.

Do Indian people pay taxes?

Individual American Indians and Alaska Natives and their businesses pay federal income tax just like all other Americans. The exception is that the income an Indian receives directly from a treaty or trust resource such as fish or timber is not federally taxed. States cannot tax tribal citizens who live on and derive their income from tribal lands, but those who work or live outside tribal lands generally are subject to state income, sales and other taxes.

Do tribal governments pay federal taxes?

Tribal government revenues are not taxed, just as state and local government revenues are not taxed. This long-standing federal policy with Constitutional support prevents interference with the ability to raise revenue for government functions.

Tribal government revenues are not taxed, just as state and local government revenues are not taxed.

Do tribal governments pay state taxes?

States cannot directly tax a tribal government. The Supreme Court has held that state governments can collect excise taxes on sales to non-tribal citizens that occur on tribal lands, so long as the tax does not fall directly on the tribal government. States and tribes have developed a variety of methods for collecting these taxes, such as intergovernmental agreements or pre-taxing at the wholesale level.

Why do tribes have immunity from lawsuits?

Government or sovereign immunity applies to state, local and federal—as well as tribal—governments. Government immunity protects government funds and discretionary government functions. Like other governments, tribes provide for insurance and limited waivers of their sovereign immunity, taking responsibility for the actions of tribal employees. No government could successfully operate without sovereign immunity to protect the discretionary actions of government officials.

Aren't all Indian tribes getting rich from casinos?

Gaming has done little to change the depressed economic conditions found on most reservations.

The media coverage of tribal gaming has left the impression that all tribes have grown rich on casino money and that poverty has been eradicated in Indian communities. In fact, only a small number of Indian tribes have found economic success through gaming. Of the 558 tribes, only 198 are engaged in gaming, and 22 of those tribes collect 56 percent of the revenue. In reality, gaming has done little to change the depressed economic conditions found on most reservations.

Does the federal government regulate Indian gaming?

In 1988, Congress formally recognized but limited the right of Indians to conduct gaming when it passed the Indian Gaming Regulatory Act (IGRA). The IGRA created the National Indian Gaming Commission to regulate Indian gaming. The IGRA generally allows tribes to use Class II games such as bingo, so long as these games are not criminally prohibited by the state. For Class III casino gaming, however, tribes first must negotiate compacts with states concerning the games to be played and the regulation required for the games.

How do Indian nations use the revenues from Indian gaming?

Like state and local governments, tribes use revenues from any source as a tax base to fund essential services such as education, law enforcement, tribal courts, health care and other social services, economic development, and infrastructure improvement. In fact, Indian tribes are required by IGRA to use their gaming revenues for such purposes. Tribal government gaming—enterprises run by government entities to raise revenues for essential government functions—is more akin to state lotteries than to commercial for-profit businesses.

3. STATE GOVERNMENTS: FOCUS ON THE LEGISLATURES

The State-Federal Relationship

The relationships between the states and the federal government were first recognized in the Articles of Confederation in 1781. The U.S. Constitution was drafted in 1787, but it was in 1791 that the Tenth Amendment was drafted.

The federal government ensures some minimum cohesiveness or commonality in the way programs and government functions are carried out across the nation, but implementation and adaptation of these programs and functions generally are left to the states. Relations between state governments and the federal government are not so simple. A complex web of responsibilities and jurisdictions often confuses the issue of where federal control ends and state control begins.

A complex web of responsibilities and jurisdictions often confuses the issue of where federal control ends and state control begins.

Geography, economics and other factors may influence the relationships states have with the federal government. States and state governments are as diverse as tribes and tribal governments. Rooted in the historical development of the country, western states, for instance, may be more independent or wary of the federal government despite—or because of—the vast federal land holdings in the west. But poorer states—wherever their location—may be more dependent on federal assistance.

The Structure of State Governments

Three branches of government exist within the states: legislative, executive and judicial. As the U.S. Constitution establishes the three branches of the federal government, state constitutions establish the three branches of state government. Having three distinct branches—a "separation of powers"—allows each to have its own responsibilities, but none to be more powerful than the others.

Legislative

The legislative function is threefold: they write the state laws, appropriate the funding, and conduct oversight to ensure that the laws are enforced and the state agencies effectively perform their duties. Under state constitutions, legislatures have general lawmaking powers. Legislatures, rather than agencies, generally make the initial political decisions that balance competing interests such as economic development and environmental protection. Agency officials are not accountable in the same way to the citizens as are elected legislators and are not compelled to make the difficult policy choices that legislatures must make.

Legislatures ultimately authorize all agency program budgets.

All branches of state government are funded by citizen taxes that are appropriated by the legislatures—in this sense the three branches are linked by this annual or biennial process. State budget processes are complex and it often takes much of the year to develop the budget. In most states, the governor is legally responsible for developing proposed budgets. He or she does so with substantial input from state agency directors, who are responsible for reporting expenditures and forecasting budget needs for their individual agencies. Most legislatures have budget review offices or agencies that monitor state spending and help prepare appropriations bills for consideration by the legislatures. Some legislatures follow the governor's budget, others may not follow it so closely. The legislatures ultimately authorize all agency program budgets and often authorize specific spending for particular items by passing a budget bill, which then must be signed by the governor.

Understanding the budget process and the role of the legislature, the governor and the agencies can help neighboring governments to effectively work with the state government.

Executive

The governor and the agencies make up the executive branch. The governor— the "chief executive" of the state—sets policy through executive orders or proclamations. Generally, a new governor can reverse those orders. The governor can propose legislation and also has veto authority over legislative actions, but legislatures, with a substantial majority, can override a governor's veto. In most states, the governor appoints agency directors. The agencies carry out laws enacted by the legislative branch by providing services, implementing non-service programs, and practicing enforcement authority as granted by the legislature. State agencies handle specific issues and have defined areas of responsibility.

Agencies carry out laws enacted by the legislative branch.

Judicial

The judiciary, or court system, in each state acts as a check on the other branches by ruling on controversies that may involve state laws and governing processes. (Most states are moving toward adopting merit systems to select judges; a few still use popular elections.) The legislature or governor can react to a court ruling with which they disagree by amending state law and policy, unless it is a constitutional issue.

The Structure of State Legislatures

The 50 state legislatures have many similar elements. All have periodic elections, establish legislative leadership and committee systems, and employ staff who assist individual members and the legislative process to run smoothly.

Forty-nine states have bicameral legislatures made up of two chambers or legislative houses called the senate and the house of representatives. In a few states, the house is officially called the assembly or house of delegates. Of the two houses, the house is generally the larger body, and members serve shorter terms than their senate counterparts. The sizes of legislatures—established in state constitutions—also vary greatly, from New Hampshire's 400-member House to Alaska's 20-member Senate.

Legislative Districts

There are 7,424 state legislators in the United States and the number of legislators who serve in each state varies dramatically. States are divided into districts, and legislators are elected from these areas to represent the district at the state legislature.

District boundaries are redrawn every 10 years based on population data and demographic information provided by the U.S. Bureau of the Census. A series of U.S. Supreme Court rulings and the federal Voting Rights Act require that a state's legislative election districts have equal population and that each district's racial and ethnic makeup does not preclude minority groups from the potential to elect candidates of their choice.

In most states, the redrawing of legislative districts—redistricting—is done by the state legislature. A state commission performs this role in a few states.

Nebraska is the only unicameral state legislature in the nation, and legislators there are called senators. The Nebraska Legislature also is unique because it is the only state legislature where members are elected on a nonpartisan basis.

Most legislatures meet every year with the exception of Arkansas, Kentucky, Montana, Nevada, North Dakota, Oregon and Texas, which meet biennially, or once every two years. Session length varies from state to state—anywhere from 30 days to several months or, in some states, until the business is done. California, Illinois, Massachusetts, Michigan, New York, Ohio, Wisconsin and the District of Columbia meet throughout the year.

Legislative Diversity

Although each state legislature is unique, there are three general types of state legislatures, based on the population of the state, the length of the session, the size of the legislative staff, and legislative salary. These three types are referred to as 1) full-time legislatures; 2) citizen legislatures; and 3) mixed or hybrid legislatures that fall somewhere between type 1 and type 2.

In full-time legislatures more legislators work only in the legislature, have larger staff, and receive higher salaries. This type of legislature is typical in larger states that have long sessions. Citizen legislatures are those where the legislators are part-time (they usually have full-time employment elsewhere), have small staffs that also may be part-time, and are paid lower salaries. This type of legislature is typical of smaller states or low-population states that have short sessions. The third category is a combination of the full-time and citizen legislatures. These legislatures generally have medium-sized staffs and receive a moderate salary. Session lengths vary among these largely Midwestern states.

Diversity exists among legislators as well. Education, subject matter expertise and experience are as varied as that of the general population. Minority groups are gaining representation in the legislatures.   Political and geographical labels do not necessarily tell all about a particular legislator. Rural members are not necessarily ultra-conservative and Democrats are not necessarily liberal, for instance.

Legislators' education, subject matter expertise and experience are as varied as that of the general population.

Term Limits

Most state house members are elected every two years, except in Alabama, Louisiana, Mississippi and Maryland, where the members serve for four years. Most senators are elected to four-year terms, except in 12 states where they have two-year terms. A recent trend in some state legislatures has been to set limits on how many terms a person may hold office as a representative or senator. Eighteen states have various term limits (most states also limit the number of terms that the governor can serve). The length of term limits varies in each of the 18 states.

Legislative Leadership

Certain members hold leadership positions in their respective legislative chambers. The top positions are the speaker for the house of representatives and the president, president pro tem or majority leader for the senate. These leaders—elected by the members of the entire chamber or a majority of their party members—usually decide committee assignments and set the overall session agendas. Leadership also can have significant influence over particular legislation.

Each chamber also has a majority (the political party with the most seats in the legislature) leader who is elected by his or her political party or appointed by the speaker or president of the respective chamber. These leaders, who are primarily responsible for scheduling bills for consideration and controlling the debate when the bill reaches the floor, work closely with the speaker or the president. Minority (the political party with less seats than the majority in the legislature) leaders represent their political party in the senate or house. Finally, majority and minority "whips" in both chambers serve as liaisons between leadership and members, and perform various functions related to their political party. Informal or unspoken power structures may include legislators who although they have no formal leadership position, serve as part of the "inner circle" of those who may wield legislative power among colleagues.

Legislative Committees

Committee hearings are open to the public, and offer an opportunity for citizens to voice opinions.

Legislative committees hear most of the debate on proposed bills. Committee hearings are open to the public, and offer an opportunity for citizens to voice opinions and explain the pros and cons of specific topics that may affect their community. Legislators depend on these hearings to learn enough about the proposed legislation to make informed decisions to vote for or against it.

All committees are either comprised of legislators from one house only, or are "joint" committees with members from both houses. Occasionally non-legislators will sit on committees. The three main types of legislative committees are standing, interim and select. Standing committees deal with broad topics such as education, local government, finance, human services and environment. They meet during the legislative session and continue from year to year. These committee members review, debate and refine legislation before any action is taken on the legislation by the entire body. Interim committees are akin to study groups that meet between sessions. They generally have a narrower focus. Select committees are similar to interim committees in that they meet on specific subjects or proposals, but they dissolve when the task is done. Both interim and select committees often are authorized at the end of the session to look at issues that were debated but not enacted.

Committee members review, debate and refine legislation before any action is taken on the legislation by the entire body.

Committees are chaired by legislators who have some expertise in or knowledge of the topic area, and are supported by legislative staff. By virtue of their jurisdiction, some committees are more powerful than others. Appropriations, ways and means, finance, and rules are among the more influential committees in most states.

Legislative Staff

The importance of staff in the legislative process should not be underestimated, because they provide information to and thus influence the legislators. Non-partisan legislative staff offices provide year-round research and legal capabilities dedicated to the legislative branch. These offices are independent of the executive branch. They provide background information on bills, respond to information requests from the members and may staff various committees of the legislature. Staff also may draft bills out of these offices or from separate legislative drafting offices. Fiscal and audit staff analyze budgets and evaluate programs.

An increasing number of professional and partisan legislative staff are being hired by state legislatures. Partisan legislative staff work exclusively for majority or minority leadership or Democratic or Republican caucuses and focus generally on developing party positions. Personal legislative staff—those who work for only one legislator—are common in larger states. All staff are responsible for assisting legislators in carrying out their duties, and some may have considerable influence on legislative action.

Staff are responsible for assisting legislators in carrying out their duties.

Chief staff officers in each chamber—the secretary of the senate and the clerk of the house—are responsible for reading bills upon introduction, preparing chamber calendars, tracking amendments, recording votes, publishing journals that reflect floor action, posting committee hearing schedules, and engrossing and enrolling bills.

Committee staff record votes and prepare minutes, amendments and committee reports. They often brief the members on the issue(s) and may assist in preparing questions that members will ask of witnesses to clarify points or address specific concerns.

Legislative Mechanisms for Addressing Tribal Issues

Legislatures have various forums and methods to address tribal issues. Several states have legislative committees—both standing and interim—dedicated to Indian affairs. These committees generally are comprised of legislators only, but they hear testimony from any interested party.

Some states have councils, committees or commissions that include appointed representatives from state administrative and legislative branches, and often from the tribes. A few states have issue-specific committees or councils, such as gaming or fisheries commissions. Finally, many states have Indian affairs commissions that are solely mechanisms of the executive branches and generally do not include legislative involvement. A complete listing of state committees and commissions is included in appendix A.

Maine has a unique mechanism. Under the state's House Rule 525, one representative each from the Penobscot Nation and the Passamaquoddy Tribe are granted seats on the floor of the house with speaking privileges. They can serve on committees, and have other legislative rights and privileges except for voting. They also may sponsor or cosponsor legislation that specifically relates to Indians and Indian land claims.

Some states have "Tribal Government Day" or "Indian Day" at the legislatures where, for instance, tribal leaders may be invited to address the legislature. Annual or regularly scheduled meetings between tribal and state legislative representatives also may be scheduled.

Lastly, legislatures have addressed Indian issues by enacting laws directing agencies or local governments to enter into intergovernmental agreements with tribes. This legislation may address the general principles and processes of entering into agreements, and may include direction to agencies or the governor to enter into agreements on specific issues in such areas such as tax, law enforcement, gaming, human services or environmental protection.

Legislatures have addressed Indian issues by enacting laws directing agencies or local governments to enter into intergovernmental agreements with tribes.

Answers to Frequently Asked Questions About State Legislatures

Who can submit legislative proposals to the state legislature?

A legislator must introduce bills and other proposals to the legislature as a whole. Anyone, however, may suggest a proposal to a legislator, who then, can present it to the body. Some states have deadlines—usually soon after the beginning of the session—for submitting proposals to the legislature to reduce the sheer number of proposals submitted and the amount of interruption of regularly scheduled business.

How are state legislative proposals written?

Proposals generally take the form of resolutions, memorials or bills. Proposals generally are written by legal specialists or lawyers on the legislature's staff. Bills drafted by people outside the legislature must be reviewed by legislative staff to ensure that they follow the correct format.

What is a bill sponsor?

A bill sponsor is a legislator who supports an idea and requests that a bill be drafted for introduction or introduces a bill that already is drafted. Many states limit the number of bills a member can introduce. Cosponsors are other legislators who agree with and support the sponsor of a bill they believe would be a good law.

What happens once a bill is introduced?

Anywhere during the process, a bill may be defeated, amended or substituted by another bill.

After a member introduces a bill in his or her chamber, it is assigned a number and then is referred to a committee(s) that may hold hearings and either report the bill back to the chamber without any changes, report an amended version, or recommend that the bill not be passed. Once through committee, a bill is placed on a calendar in the house or the senate, where it is debated and passed or defeated by a majority vote. It then is sent to the other chamber where the same process is followed. If it passes both chambers, the bill goes to the governor, who either signs or vetoes the legislation. Anywhere during this process, the bill may be defeated, amended or substituted by another bill.

How do you find out about committee times, agendas and bill status?

Committees meet in various rooms throughout the state capitol. The times and locations are posted in various places within the capitol, on the state legislative web site, and may be advertised in the statewide newspapers.

Calendars and agendas are the schedules of business for each day in each chamber and for committees. Floor calendars are set by the speaker of the house or the senate president. Committee chairs set committee agendas. To obtain notices regarding the agendas for a particular day's floor session or a committee meeting, contact the legislative information number (appendix D) for referral to the correct office in that state.

Bill status can be obtained by calling the bill status phone numbers (appendix D). In addition, most state legislative web sites can be searched for bills in each session by subject, keyword, sponsor or bill number. Some state web pages are more up-to-date than others.

Who can address a senate or house of representatives?

Unlike legislative committee hearings, only legislators and staff generally are allowed access to the floor of either chamber to address the members. Simple introductions by a legislator of a guest either on the floor or in the gallery (the public seating area above the floor) are common. However, it is extremely rare that a non-legislator is allowed to address the floor. The only way to obtain permission to address a chamber of the legislature is to approach a legislator or the presiding officer— the speaker or the president—and make a request. Such requests must be made well in advance and may very well be rejected. Even the governor can address a chamber only by special invitation.

Only legislators and staff generally are allowed access to the floor of either chamber to address the members.

4. WORKING WITH NEIGHBORING GOVERNMENTS

Often, the knowledge of how an entity is structured and why it operates as it does is not enough to help understand why and how to actually work with that entity. This chapter offers not only considerations of the potential reasons to work together and the benefits of collaboration, but also provides suggestions about how to initiate contact and build relationships.

Why Work With Tribal Governments?

In areas of overlapping or adjacent jurisdiction, states and tribes can realize significant benefits from cooperation.

As sovereign governments, tribes and states often have similar issues of concern. Both are responsible for their constituencies—providing needed programs and services, using limited resources effectively, and promoting sustainable development. In areas of overlapping or adjacent jurisdiction, states and tribes can realize significant benefits from cooperation.

Tribal governments know their constituents; they provide a variety of programs and services. Tribal governments often can more successfully provide effective, appropriate services to tribal citizens and can coordinate state-provided services with services that already are provided on the reservation to ensure comprehensive, non-duplicative services. Tribal governments themselves are the fundamental source of authority in Indian

Country, and it is best to contact them directly regarding concerns or questions about a tribal matter. NCAI and other tribal organizations can serve as a resource, but are no substitute for direct communication with tribal governments.

How to Work Effectively With Tribal Governments

The more than 558 tribal governments are listed in appendix C. A complete list of federally recognized tribes with addresses and phone numbers also is available on the NCAI web site (www.ncai.org). If your state has a commission, office or committee on Indian affairs (appendix A) or an intertribal association (appendix B), these can serve as key resources to assist in contacting tribal officials and understanding the governmental structure and protocols that are unique to each tribe.

In general, it is best to communicate and coordinate with tribal governments on a *government-to-government* basis, in a manner similar to the relationships between other state or federal government agencies. It is recommended that coordination take place as early as possible and before any official notifications are made. A key is ongoing, long-term relationships, where communication continually is shared and updated. Several states have developed agreements and protocols on state-tribal communication and coordination that have been helpful in regularizing the contacts between states and tribes.

It is best to communicate and coordinate with tribal governments on a government-to-government basis.

In contacting a tribal government, it is generally appropriate to contact (by letter, phone or fax) the chief executive of the tribe. In matters concerning a particular issue (i.e., roads, social service delivery or natural resources), it also is also appropriate to contact the responsible tribal program director, but it is important to understand the structure of each tribe, and to notify the chief executive of the tribe in regard to all important issues.

Beyond these general observations, it is essential to understand the structure of the tribal government in order to successfully coordinate with a specific tribe. For example, some tribal governments have distinct executive and legislative branches, so it may be important to communicate with both branches. Other tribes have a system more akin to parliament, where the chief executive also is the chair of the tribal council. In these cases, communicating with the chairperson may be effective for communicating with the entire tribal government.

Tribal governments share many characteristics with other forms of government so the process of initiating contacts should be familiar. Because tribal officials have been elected or appointed to serve their citizens, it is entirely appropriate to open communication on matters that may be of concern to the tribal community.

Why Work With State Legislators?

Many issues can and should be addressed at the legislative level.

Many tribal representatives may be used to working with state executive branch officials, whether with the governor or with agency personnel. However, many issues can and should be addressed at the legislative level. In a nutshell, here are some reasons to get to know state legislators and legislatures.

- Indian issues can be addressed through legislation that is drafted by people familiar with the issues. Legislation that is drafted by those who have inadequate knowledge or information about an issue may have unintended adverse effects on tribes and may fail to accomplish the intended goals.
- Legislative policy is likely to be longer lasting than executive branch policy, which can change with every administration.
- Individual legislators are accessible.
- Legislators are close to the people, have a relatively small member-to-constituent ratio, and have a working knowledge of local conditions.

- Mutual education—of tribal leaders about the legislative process and of legislators about tribal government and the realities of Indian country—is facilitated by state legislator-tribal leader relationships.
- Legislatures are responsible for appropriating funds for all state-funded programs.

Specifically, individual legislators sponsor, amend and vote on bills that provide services to and appropriations for the entire state. Legislative staff can be instrumental in the process because they conduct the research, may draft the bills and amendments, and are responsible for the smooth operation of the legislature during its sessions. In many states, legislative staff specialize in particular topic areas.

Legislators are elected to represent their constituents' best interests. The current trend of devolution means the states—and, in some cases, the tribes—are taking on different and additional responsibilities. This will affect not only Indian tribes and communities, but also the state-tribal relationship. The legislatures are in a key position to enact effective (or ineffective) policies.

If individual legislators are unaware of particular needs within their district or the state as a whole, they cannot address the problem through legislation. Knowing the legislators who represent your district and knowing the state legislative lead-

---

A Note on State Agencies

For the majority of state government issues that tribes might encounter, a state agency is designated to handle the matter. State agencies are created by state legislatures to handle the day-to-day business of state government. For transportation projects, building inspections, emergency response planning, leaking underground storage tanks, Medicaid reimbursement, discriminatory lending practices, tax collection, job training, tourism promotion, criminal enforcement, and a host of other specific issues, a state agency or commission generally is responsible, and there may be a local office that can deal with your issue. In many instances, it is most efficient and effective to work through the appropriate state agency, as long as the legislature has granted that agency the authority and funding to handle the particular issue.

State agency addresses and phone numbers are listed in the blue pages of the phone book, or usually can be found on the state web site at "www.state. (two letter state initials).us". It is worth the time to learn about the state agencies, their functions, and the services they can provide.

ership are first steps in establishing the necessary working relationships.

How to Work Effectively With State Legislators

Understanding the legislative process—much of which is described in chapter 3—is imperative to successful working relationships. Equally as important is an understanding of the
politics of the state in general and within the legislature. Political party and individual legislator agendas, the make-up of
the legislature in terms of party divisions, and any dissension
between or within the parties all are useful to understand. If
there are party differences or other sources of disagreement
between the legislature and the governor know who must sign
bills. Work with members of both the majority and minority,
and be aware of election dates. The closer to an election, the
more likely legislators will follow partisan platforms.

It is especially important to work on building personal relationships with legislators and staff,

Personal contact with legislators often is the most effective.
Visits at the capitol during session might be necessary, but
legislators often are more accessible when the legislature is not
in session. It is especially important to work on building personal relationships with legislators and staff, instead of visiting
them only when their support is needed.

Understand the committee process as well as what happens to
bills on chamber floors. Be aware of committee meetings or
hearings on topics relevant to you or your community, so that
you can attend them, voice your opinion, and clearly state
why you support or oppose a proposal. Be prepared and well-
versed so that you can state your concerns clearly. Prepare a
short written summary of your position so that legislators can
take it with them to review later. The more you work with the
committees, the better the legislators will get to know you
and understand your positions, as well as the common goals
and needs that your tribe shares with the state.

This advice is applicable to any person or group who has a stake in the outcomes of the legislative process. Tribal leaders will want to consider how the legislature may perceive those tribal representatives who act in a lobbying capacity before the legislature. Appearing as a special interest, although at times unavoidable in protecting your communities, may not afford you the same respect as if you were to approach the legislature on a government-to-government basis. Some legislative mechanisms that may assist in developing a government-to-government relationship are discussed in chapter 3.

Tribal governments deal with many issues about which state governments also are concerned. Although many issues tribes have may be more effectively dealt with at the agency level, the agency may not have either the authority or the direction to work with tribes. Being involved in the legislative process is a good way to begin to coordinate with the state on issues that are of concern to all.

Being involved in the legislative process is a good way to begin to coordinate with the state on issues that are of concern to all.

5. CONCLUSION

Misunderstandings often arise from a lack of understanding. A first step to good relations is knowing how neighboring governments operate and what issues are important to them. The primary prerequisite for cooperation between governments is a mutual understanding of the unique circumstances, needs and overall culture within which each government operates. The National Conference of State Legislatures and the National Congress of American Indians are working toward mutual education on governmental function and structure. This guide represents a beginning. Additional efforts of these organizations and many others—as well as state and tribal leaders themselves—ultimately will promote greater state-tribal cooperation in general, and also in substantive program areas such as protecting the environment, managing natural resources and implementing welfare reform.

An increased tribal and state capacity to address mutual issues will result in more open and productive long-term relationships.

The pace of state-tribal activity is expected to increase due to the devolution of the federal government's historical responsibilities to state and tribal governments. There are several ways to address the current situation and prepare for the future consequences of this trend. The compilation and dissemination of information, dialogue among state and tribal leaders who have common interests, and an increased capacity of tribes and states to address mutual issues will result in more open and productive long-term relationships.

It is important that all stakeholders work toward institutionalization of the positive relationships that exist and continue

38

to be formed. Changing social and economic conditions and political turnover threaten any political relationship, but permanent forums and communication channels can help state and tribal leaders face challenges of mutual interest. No government can operate effectively unless it coordinates with neighboring governments. By collaborating on issues of mutual concern, states and tribes have the opportunity to improve governance and better serve their respective constituents.

No government can operate effectively unless it coordinates with neighboring governments.

Appendix A. State Committees and Commissions on Indian Affairs

Alabama
Indian Affairs Commission
(334) 242-2830
Darla F. Graves, Executive Director
http://www.archives.state.al.us/agencies/indicom
.html

Alaska
Rural Government Task Force
Staff, Andy_Ebona@gov.state.ak.us

Arizona
House Rural and Native American Affairs
Committee (L)
http://www.azleg.state.az.us/committe/44leg/
hrnaa.min.htm

Commission on Indian Affairs
(602) 542-3123
Ron S. Lee, Executive Director
http://www.indianaffairs.state.az.us

Arkansas
None

California
Assembly Select Committee on Indian
Gaming (L)
Assembly Select Committee on Native American
Repatriation (L)

Native American Heritage Commission
(916) 653-4082
Larry Myers, Executive Secretary

Office of Native American Affairs
(877) 860-2863
Olin Jones, Director

Colorado
Commission of Indian Affairs
(303) 866-3027
Karen D. Wilde-Rogers, Executive Secretary
http://www.state.co.us/gov_dir/ltgov/indian/
indian.htm

Connecticut
Office of American Indian Affairs
(860) 424-3066
Ed Sarabia, Indian Affairs Coordinator

This list is available and updated on NCSL's web site at http://www.ncsl.org/programs/esnr/stlegcom.htm. For legislative committee ("L") phone numbers, call the general information numbers listed for the legislatures in appendix D.

Delaware
Nanticoke Indian Association
(302) 945-3400
Kenneth Clark, Director

Florida
Governor's Council on Indian Affairs Inc.
(850) 488-0730
(800) 322-9186
Joe A. Quetone, Executive Director
http://www.fgcia.com

Georgia
Council on American Indian Concerns
(404) 656-6527
Billy Thompson
Nealie McCormick, Chairman

Hawaii
House Committee on Judiciary and
    Hawaiian Affairs (L)

Senate Committee on Water, Land and
    Hawaiian Affairs (L)

Office of Hawaiian Affairs
(808) 594-1888
Randall K. Ogata, Administrator

Idaho
Council on Indian Affairs
Mike McConnell, staff
(208) 334-2475

Illinois
American Indian Center
(773) 275-5871
http://www.mcs.net/~aic
Maxine Spatari, Executive Director

Indiana
Civil Rights Commission
(317) 232-6549
(800) 628-2909
http://www.ai.org/icrc
Sandra D. Leek, Director

Iowa
None

Kansas
Joint Committee on State-Tribal Relations (L)

Native American Affairs
(785) 368-7319
Brad Hamilton, Director

Kentucky
None

Louisiana
Governor's Office of Indian Affairs
(225) 219-7556
Pat Arnould, Deputy Director
http://www.indianaffairs.com/

Maine
Indian Tribal State Commission
(207) 622-4815
Diane C. Scully, Executive Director

Maryland
Commission on Indian Affairs
(410) 514-7653
Elaine Eff, Acting Administrator

Massachusetts
Commission on Indian Affairs
(617) 727-6966
John A. Peters Jr. Executive Director

Michigan
American Indian Affairs Office
(517) 241-7748
Donna Budnick, American Indian Specialist

Minnesota
Indian Affairs Council
(218) 755-3825
Joe Day, Executive Director
http://www.indians.state.mn.us

Mississippi
None

Missouri
None

Montana
Law, Justice & Indian Affairs Committee (L)

Office of Indian Affairs
(406) 444-3713

Nebraska
Commission on Indian Affairs
(402) 471-3475
Judi Morgan, Executive Director

Nevada
Indian Commission
(775) 688-1347
http://www.ael.org/eric/ned/ned287.htm
Sherrada James, Executive Director

New Hampshire
None

New Jersey
Commission on Native American Affairs
(609) 777-2869

New Mexico
Joint (House/Senate) Indian Affairs Committee
(L)

Senate Indian and Cultural Affairs Committee
(L)

Joint Legislative Committee on Compacts (L)

Office of Indian Affairs
(505) 827-6440
Regis Pecos, Executive Director

New York
State Office of Children and Family Services—
Indian Affairs
(716) 847-3123
Kim M. Thomas, Indian Affairs Specialist

North Carolina
House Military, Veterans, and Indian Affairs
Committee (L)

Commission on Indian Affairs
(919) 733-5998
http://www.doa.state.nc.us/cia/welcome.htm
Gregory Richardson, Executive Director

North Dakota
Indian Affairs Commission
(701) 328-2428
http://www.health.state.nd.us/ndiac/
Cynthia Mala, Executive Director

Ohio
None

Oklahoma
Joint Committee on State-Tribal Relations (L)

Indian Affairs Commission
(405) 521-3828
http://www.state.ok.us/~oiac
Barbara A. Warner, Executive Director

Oregon
Legislative Commission on Indian Services (L)
(503) 986-1068
http://www.leg.state.or.us/cis/cisset.htm
Karen Quigley, Executive Director

Rhode Island
Joseph S. Larison Jr.
Governor's Executive Counsel
(401) 222-2080

South Carolina
None

South Dakota
State-Tribal Relations Interim Committee (L)

Office of Tribal Government Relations
(605) 773-3415
Webster Two Hawk Sr. Commissioner

Tennessee
Commission of Indian Affairs
(615) 532-0745
http://www.state.tn.us/environment/cia/
    index.html
Toye Heape, Executive Director

Texas
None

Utah
Native American Legislative Liaison Committee
(L)

Division of Indian Affairs
(801) 538-8808
http://www.dced.state.ut.us/Indian/About_us/
    staff.html
Forrest S. Cuch, Executive Director

Vermont
Governor's Advisory Commission on Native
American Affairs
(802) 868-4033
Jeff Benay, Chairman

Virginia
Council on Indians
(804) 697-6342
http://www.indians.vipnet.org/index.html
Chief Barry Bass, Acting Chairman

Washington
Working Group on State-Tribal Legislative
    Relations
Alan Parker
(360) 866-6000

Governor's Office of Indian Affairs
(360) 753-2411
Kimberly Craven, Executive Director

West Virginia
None

Wisconsin
Special Committee on State-Tribal Relations (L)

Wyoming
Indian Affairs Council
(307) 432-0380
Gary Maier, Wyoming Community Services
Manager and Indian Affairs Councilman

Appendix B. National and Regional Tribal Organizations

National Tribal Organizations

American Indian Higher Education Council
(703) 838-0400
www.aihec.org

American Indian Resources Institute
(510) 834-9333

Council of Energy Resource Tribes
(303) 282-7576

First Nations Development Institute
(540) 371-5615
www.firstnations.org

Indian and Native American Employment and
    Training Coalition
(907) 265-5975

Inter-Tribal Agricultural Council
(406) 259-3525

Inter-Tribal Timber Council
(503) 282-4296
www.teleport.com/~itc1/index.html

Inter-Tribal Transportation Association
(918) 287-1128

National American Indian Court Judges
    Association
(860) 396-6319
www.naicja.org

National American Indian Housing Council
(202) 789-1754
naihc.Indian.com

National Congress of American Indians
(202) 466-7767
 www.ncai.org

National Indian Business Association
(202) 547-0580

National Indian Child Care Association
(918) 758-1463
www.nicca.org

National Indian Child Welfare Association
(503) 222-4044
www.nicwa.org

National Indian Council on Aging
(505) 292-2001
www.nicoa.org

National Indian Education Association
(703) 838-2870
www.niea.org

National Indian Gaming Association
(202) 546-7711
www.niga.org

National Indian Health Board
(303) 759-3075
www.nihb.org

National Indian Justice Center
(707) 762-8113
nijc.indian.com

National Native American AIDS Prevention
   Center
(510) 444-2051
www.nnaapc.org

National Tribal Environmental Council
(505) 242-2175
www.ntec.org

Native American Rights Fund
(202) 785-4166
www.narf.org

Regional Inter-Tribal Organizations

Affiliated Tribes of Northwest Indians
(503) 241-0070
www.atni.org

Alaska Inter-Tribal Council
(907) 563-9334
www.aitc.org

Alaska Federation of Natives
(907) 274-3611
www.ankn.uaf.edu

All Indian Pueblo Council
(505) 881-1992

Association of Village Council Presidents
(907) 543-3521

California Council of Tribal Governments
(530) 244-2994

California Indian Manpower Consortium
(916) 920-0285

Great Lakes Inter-Tribal Council
(715) 588-3324
www.newnorth.net/glitc/glitc.htm

Inter-Tribal Council of the Five Civilized Tribes
(918) 756-8700

Inter-Tribal Council of Nevada
(702) 355-0600
www.itcn.org

Inter-Tribal Council of Arizona
(602) 248-0071
www.primenet.com/~itca

Inter-Tribal Council of California
(916) 973-9581

Michigan Inter-Tribal Council
(906) 632-6896

Midwest Alliance of Sovereign Tribes
(320) 532-4181

Montana-Wyoming Tribal Leaders Council
(406) 252-2550
tlc.wtp.net

Northwest Portland Area Indian Health Board
(503) 228-4185
www.npaihb.org

Oklahomans for Indian Opportunity
(405) 329-3737

Southern California Tribal
    Chairman's Association
(760) 749-0910

United Tribes of Texas, Kansas and
    Oklahoma
(918) 968-3526

United South and Eastern Tribes
(615) 872-7900
one/web.org/oneida/uset/uset.html

APPENDIX C. NATIONAL AND REGIONAL STATE ORGANIZATIONS AND WEB SITES

General State Organizations and Web Sites

American Legislative Exchange Council (ALEC)
(202) 466-3800
www.alec.org

Data Web Sites for the 50 States
www.prb.org/news/stateweb.htm

Governing Magazine
www.governing.com/state.htm

Council of State Governments (CSG)
(859) 244-8000
www.statesnews.org

National Association of Attorneys General (NAAG)
(202) 326-6000
www.naag.org/index2.html

National Association of Secretaries of State
(202) 624-3525
www.nass.org/

National Conference of State Legislatures (NCSL)
(303) 830-2200
www.ncsl.org/

National Governors' Association (NGA)
(202) 624-5346
http://nga.org

Ohio-Kentucky-Indiana Regional Council of Governments
(513) 621-6300
www.oki.org/

Politics: Project Vote Smart
www.vote-smart.org/

State Courts Directory
www.piperinfo.com/pl03/statedir.html

49

State Law
www.alllaw.com/state_resources/
state_law_search/

Stateline (PEW Research Center)
www.stateline.org/

States.org
www.states.org/

Western Governors Association (WGA)
(303) 623-9378 or (202) 624-5402
www.westgov.org

Subject-Specific Organizations and Web Sites

American Association of State and Highway
Transportation
(202) 624-5800
www.aashto.org/

Appalachian Regional Commission (ARC)
(202) 884-7799
http://arc.gov/

Education Commission for the States
(303) 299-3600
www.ecs.org/ecs/ecsweb.nsf/

Environmental Council of the States
(202) 624-3660
http://www.sso.org/ecos/

Federation of State Medical Boards
(817) 868-4000
www.fsmb.org/

Governors' Interstate Indian Council (GIIC)
www.state.ok.us/~oiac/giic.html

Great Lakes Commission
(734) 665-9135
www.glc.org

Hate Crimes Statutes (Hate Crimes Prevention
Center)
www.civilrights.org/lcef/hateam/

Insurance News Network: State Insurance
Gateway
(860) 233-2800
www.insure.com/states/index.html

Interstate Oil and Gas Compact Commission
(405) 525-3556
www.iogcc.oklaosf.state.ok.us/

Multistate Tax Commission
(202) 624-8699
www.mtc.gov/

National Assembly of State Art Agencies
(202) 347-6352
www.nasaa-arts.org/

National Association of Regulatory Utility
Commissioners
(202) 898-2200
www.naruc.org/

National Association of State Auditors,
Comptrollers and Treasurers
(606) 276-1147
www.sso.org/nasact/nasact.htm

National Association of State Budget Officers
202-624-5382
www.nasbo.org/

National Association of State Departments of
Agriculture
(202) 296-9680
www.nasda-hq.org/

National Association of State Information
Resource Executives
(859) 231-1971
www.nasire.org/

National Center for State Courts
(757) 253-2000
www.ncsc.dni.us/

South Atlantic Fishery Management Council
(843) 571-4366
www.safmc.nmfs.gov/

State Libraries
(608) 266-2127
www.dpi.state.wi.us/dpi/dlcl/pld/statelib.html

State Science and Technology Institute (SSTI)
(614) 901-1690
www.ssti.org/

Women Executives in State Government
(202) 628-9374
www.wesg.org/contact.htm

State Genetics Laws (NCSL)
www.ncsl.org/programs/employ/Genetics/sg-law.htm

APPENDIX D. STATE LEGISLATIVE PHONE NUMBERS

Alabama
Alabama State House
11 S. Union St.
Montgomery, AL 36130
House info. (334) 242-4759
House bill status (334) 242-7627
Senate info. (334) 242-7800
Senate bill status (334) 242-7825

Alaska
State Capitol
120 4ᵗʰ St.
Juneau, AK 99801-1182
General Info. and bill status (907) 465-4648

Arizona
State Capitol
1700 W. Washington St.
Phoenix, AZ 85007
General info. (602) 542-4900
House bill status (602) 542-4221
Senate bill status (602) 542-3559

Arkansas
State Capitol
1500 W. Capitol Ave.
Little Rock, AR 72201
General info. (501) 682-3000
House bill status (501) 682-7771
Senate bill status (501) 682-2902

California
State Capitol
Sacramento, CA 95814
General info. (916) 657-9900
House bill status (916) 445-3614
Senate bill status (916) 445-4251

Colorado
State Capitol
200 E. Colfax Ave.
Denver, CO 80203
General info. (303) 866-5000
Bill status (303) 866-3055 or (303) 866-3521

Connecticut
State Capitol
Legislative Office Building
Hartford, CT 06106
General info. (860) 240-0100
Bill status (860) 566-4601

Delaware
Legislative Hall
P.O. Box 1401
Dover, DE 19901
General info. (302) 739-4114
Bill status (302) 739-4114

Florida

The Capitol
Tallahassee, FL 32399
General info. (850) 488-1234
Bill status (850) 488-4371

Georgia

State Capitol
Atlanta, GA 30334
General info. (404) 656-2000
House bill status (404) 656-5015
Senate bill status (404) 656-5042

Hawaii

State Capitol
415 S. Beretania St.
Honolulu, HI 96813
General info. (808) 587-0221
Bill status (808) 587-0700

Idaho

State Capitol Building
P.O. Box 83720
Boise, ID 83270
General info. (208) 332-1000
Bill status (208) 334-3175

Illinois

State House
2nd & Capitol St.
Springfield, IL 62706
General info. (217) 782-2000
Bill status (217) 782-3944

Indiana

State House
200 W. Washington St.
Indianapolis, IN 46204
General info. (317) 232-1000
Bill status (317) 232-9856

Iowa

State Capitol
Des Moines, IA 50319
General info. (515) 281-5011
Bill status (515) 281-5129

Kansas

State Capitol Building
300 SW 10th St.
Topeka, KS 66612-1504
General info. (785) 296-0111
Bill status (785) 296-3296

Kentucky

State Capitol
Capitol Ave.
Frankfort, KY 40601
General info. (502) 564-2611
Bill status (502) 564-8100

Louisiana

Secretary of State
P.O. Box 94125
Baton Rouge, LA 70804-9125
General info. (225) 342-4479
Bill status (225) 342-2456

Maine

State House Station
Augusta, ME 04333-0002
General info. (207) 287-1692
Bill status (207) 287-1692

Maryland

State House
State Circle
Annapolis, MD 21401-1991
General info. (410) 841-3000
Bill status (410) 946-5400

Massachusetts

State House
Boston, MA 02133
General info. (617) 722-2000
House bill status (617) 722-2356
Senate bill status (617) 722-1276

Michigan
State Capitol
100 Capitol Ave.
Lansing, MI 48909
General info. (517) 373-0184
Bill status (517) 373-0169

Minnesota
State Capitol
St. Paul, MN 55155-1606
General info. (651) 296-6013
House bill status (651) 296-6646
Senate bill status (651) 296-0504

Mississippi
State Capitol Building
P.O. Box 1018
Jackson, MS 39215-1018
General info. (601) 359-3770
Bill status (601) 359-3719 or (601) 359-3358

Missouri
State Capitol
201 W. Capitol Ave.
Jefferson City, MO 65101
General info. (573) 751-2000
Bill status (573) 751-4633

Montana
Montana Legislative Services Division
State Capitol, Room 138
P.O. Box 201706
Helena, MT 59620-1706
General info. (406) 444-2511
Bill status (406) 444-4800 or (406) 444-3064

Nebraska
2018 State Capitol
P.O. Box 94604
Lincoln, NE 68509
General info. (402) 471-2271
Bill status (402) 471-2709

Nevada
Legislative Office Building
401 S. Carson St.
Carson City, NV 89701-4747
General info. (775) 687-6825
Bill status (775) 687-5545 or (775) 687-6827

New Hampshire
State House
107 N. Main St.
Concord, NH 03301
General info. (603) 271-1110
Bill status (603) 271-2239

New Jersey
State House
Trenton, NJ 08625-0068
General info. and bill status (800) 792-8630
Bill status (609) 292-4840

New Mexico
State Capitol
Santa Fe, NM 87501
General info. and bill status
(505) 986-4600

New York
State Capitol
Albany, NY 12224
General info. (518) 474-2121
Bill status (518) 455-7545

North Carolina
State Legislative Building
16 W. Jones St.
Raleigh, NC 27601
General info. (919) 733-4111
Bill status (919) 733-7779

North Dakota
State Capitol
600 E. Boulevard Ave.
Bismarck, ND 58505-0360
General info. (701) 328-2000
Bill status (701) 328-2900 or (701) 328-2916

Ohio
State House
Columbus, OH 43215
General info. (614) 466-2000
Bill status (614) 466-8842

Oklahoma
State Capitol
2300 N. Lincoln Blvd.
Oklahoma City, OK 73105
General info. (405) 521-2011
Bill status (405) 521-5642

Oregon
State Capitol
900 Court St., NE
Salem, OR 97310
General info. (503) 986-1848
Bill status (503) 986-1180

Pennsylvania
Main Capitol Building
Harrisburg, PA 17120
General info. (717) 787-2121
Bill status (717) 787-2342

Rhode Island
State House
Providence, RI 02903
General info. (401) 222-2653
Bill status (401) 751-8833

South Carolina
State House
1200 Gervais St.
Columbia, SC 29201
House general info. (803) 734-2010
Senate general info. (803) 212-6200
Bill status (803) 734-2060

South Dakota
State Capitol
500 E. Capitol Ave.
Pierre, SD 57501
General info. (605) 773-3011
Bill status (605) 773-4498

Tennessee
Legislative Plaza
Nashville, TN 37243
General info. (800) 443-8366
Bill status (615) 741-3511

Texas
House
P.O. Box 2910
Austin, TX 78768
General info. (512) 463-0845

Senate
P.O. Box 12068
Austin, TX 78711-2068
General info. (512) 463-0100

Bill status (512) 463-2182 or (512) 463-1252

Utah
State Capitol
Salt Lake City, UT 84114
General info. (801) 538-3000
Bill status (801) 538-1588

Vermont
State House
115 State St. Drawer 33
Montpelier, VT 05633-5301
General info. (802) 828-2331
Bill status (802) 828-2231

Virginia
State Capitol
P.O. Box 406
Richmond, VA 23218
General info. (804) 786-0000
Bill status (804) 698-1500

Washington
House
P.O. Box 40600
Olympia, WA 98504-0600
General info. (360) 786-7750

Senate
P.O. Box 40482
Olympia, WA 98504-0482
General info. (360) 786-7550

Bill status (800) 562-6000 or (360) 786-7573

West Virginia
State Capitol
Charleston, WV 25305
General info. (304) 558-3456
Bill status (304) 347-4836

Wisconsin
State Capitol
Madison, WI 53702
General info. (608) 266-2211
Bill status (608) 266-9960

Wyoming
State Capitol
Cheyenne, WY 82002
General info. (307) 777-7881
Bill status (307) 777-6185 or (307) 777-7881

APPENDIX E. LIST OF FEDERALLY AND STATE-RECOGNIZED TRIBES

Alabama

Federally Recognized
Poarch Band of Creeks

State-Recognized
Mowa Band of Choctaws
Echota Cherokees
Cherokees of S.E. Alabama
MaChis Lower Alabama Creek Tribe
Star Clan-Muscogee Creek Tribe
Cherokees of N.E. Alabama

Alaska

Federally Recognized
Village of Afognak
Native Village of Akhiok
Akiachak Native Community
Akiak Native Community
Native Village of Akutan
Village of Alakanuk
Alatna Village
Native Village of Aleknagik
Algaaciq Native Village (St. Mary's)
Allakaket Village
Native Village of Ambler

Village of Anaktuvuk Pass
Yupiit of Andreafski
Angoon Community Association
Village of Aniak
Anvik Village
Arctic Village (See Native Village of Venetie
    Tribal Government)
Native Village of Atka
Asa'carsarmiut Tribe (formerly Native Village of
    Mountain Village)
Atqasuk Village (Atkasook)
Village of Atmautluak
Native Village of Barrow Inupiat Traditional
    Government (formerly Native Village of
    Barrow)
Beaver Village
Native Village of Belkofski
Village of Bill Moore's Slough
Birch Creek Village
Native Village of Brevig Mission
Native Village of Buckland
Native Village of Cantwell
Native Village of Chanega (Chenega)
Chalkyitsik Village
Village of Chefornak
Chevak Native Village
Chickaloon Native Village

Native Village of Chignik
Native Village of Chignik Lagoon
Chignik Lake Village
Chilkat Indian Village (Kluckwan)
Chilkoot Indian Association (Haines)
Chinik Eskimo Community (Golovin)
Native Village of Chistochina
Native Village of Chitina
Native Village of Chuathbaluk (Russian Mission, Kuskokwim)
Chuloonawick Native Village
Circle Native Community
Village of Clark's Point
Native Village of Council
Craig Community Association
Village of Crooked Creek
Curyung Tribal Council (formerly Native Village of Dillingham)
Native Village of Deering
Native Village of Diomede (Inalik)
Village of Dot Lake
Douglas Indian Association
Native Village of Eagle
Native Village of Eek
Egegik Village
Eklutna Native Village
Native Village of Ekuk
Ekwok Village
Native Village of Elim
Emmonak Village
Evansville Village (Bettles Field)
Native Village of Eyak (Cordova)
Native Village of False Pass
Native Village of Fort Yukon
Native Village of Gakona
Galena Village (Louden Village)
Native Village of Gambell
Native Village of Georgetown
Native Village of Goodnews Bay
Organized Village of Grayling (Holikachuk)
Gulkana Village
Native Village of Hamilton
Healy Lake Village
Holy Cross Village
Hoonah Indian Association
Native Village of Hooper Bay

Hughes Village
Huslia Village
Hydaburg Cooperative Association
Igiugig Village
Village of Iliamna
Inupiat Community of the Arctic Slope
Iqurmuit Traditional Council (formerly Native Village of Russian Mission)
Ivanoff Bay Village
Kaguyak Village
Organized Village of Kake
Kaktovik Village (Barter Island)
Village of Kalskag
Village of Kaltag
Native Village of Kanatak
Native Village of Karluk
Organized Village of Kasaan
Native Village of Kasigluk
Kenaitze Indian Tribe
Ketchikan Indian Corporation
Native Village of Kiana
Agdaagux Tribe of King Cove
King Island Native Community
Native Village of Kipnuk
Native Village of Kivalina
Klawock Cooperative Association
Native Village of Kluti Kaah (Copper Center)
Knik Tribe
Native Village of Kobuk
Kokhanok Village
New Koliganek Village Council (formerly Koliganek Village)
Native Village of Kongiganak
Village of Kotlik
Native Village of Kotzebue
Native Village of Koyuk
Koyukuk Native Village
Organized Village of Kwethluk
Native Village of Kwigillingok
Native Village of Kwinhagak (Quinhagak)
Native Village of Larsen Bay
Levelock Village
Lesnoi Village (Woody Island)
Lime Village
Village of Lower Kalskag
Manley Hot Springs Village

Manokotak Village
Native Village of Marshall (Fortuna Ledge)
Native Village of Mary's Igloo
McGrath Native Village
Native Village of Mekoryuk
Mentasta Traditional Council (formerly
    Mentasta Lake Village)
Metlakatla Indian Community, Annette Island
    Reserve
Native Village of Minto
Naknek Native Village
Native Village of Nanwalek (English Bay)
Native Village of Napaimute
Native Village of Napakiak
Native Village of Napaskiak
Native Village of Nelson Lagoon
Nenana Native Association
New Stuyahok Village
Newhalen Village
Newtok Village
Native Village of Nightmute
Nikolai Village
Native Village of Nikolski
Ninilchik Village
Native Village of Noatak
Nome Eskimo Community
Nondalton Village
Noorvik Native Community
Northway Village
Native Village of Nuiqsut (Nooiksut)
Nulato Village
Native Village of Nunapitchuk
Village of Ohogamiut
Village of Old Harbor
Orutsararmuit Native Village (Bethel)
Oscarville Traditional Village
Native Village of Ouzinkie
Native Village of Paimiut
Pauloff Harbor Village
Pedro Bay Village
Native Village of Perryville
Petersburg Indian Association
Native Village of Pilot Point
Pilot Station Traditional Village
Native Village of Pitka's Point
Platinum Traditional Village

Native Village of Point Hope
Native Village of Point Lay
Native Village of Port Graham
Native Village of Port Heiden
Native Village of Port Lions
Portage Creek Village (Ohgsenakale)
Pribilof Islands Aleut Communities of St. Paul
    and St. George Islands
Qagan Toyagungin Tribe of Sand Point Village
Rampart Village
Village of Red Devil
Native Village of Ruby
Village of Salamatoff
Organized Village of Saxman
Native Village of Savoonga
Saint George (See Pribilof Islands Aleut
    Communities of St. Paul and St. George
    Islands)
Native Village of Saint Michael
Saint Paul (See Pribilof Islands Aleut
    Communities of St. Paul and St. George
    Islands)
Native Village of Scammon Bay
Native Village of Selawik
Seldovia Village Tribe
Shageluk Native Village
Native Village of Shaktoolik
Native Village of Sheldon's Point
Native Village of Shishmaref
Native Village of Shungnak
Sitka Tribe of Alaska
Skagway Village
Village of Sleetmute
Village of Solomon
South Naknek Village
Stebbins Community Association
Native Village of Stevens
Village of Stony River
Takotna Village
Native Village of Tanacross
Native Village of Tanana
Native Village of Tatitlek
Native Village of Tazlina
Telida Village
Native Village of Teller
Native Village of Tetlin

Central Council of the Tlingit and Haida Indian
Tribes
Traditional Village of Togiak
Native Village of Toksook Bay
Tuluksak Native Community
Native Village of Tuntutuliak
Native Village of Tununak
Twin Hills Village
Native Village of Tyonek
Ugashik Village
Umkumiute Native Village
Native Village of Unalakleet
Qawalangin Tribe of Unalaska
Native Village of Unga
Village of Venetie (See Native Village of Venetie
Tribal Government)
Native Village of Venetie Tribal Government
(Arctic Village and Village of Venetie)
Village of Wainwright
Native Village of Wales
Native Village of White Mountain
Wrangell Cooperative Association
Yakutat Tlingit Tribe

Arizona

Federally Recognized
Ak Chin Indian Community
Cocopah Tribe
Colorado River Indian Tribes (Arizona and
California)
Fort McDowell Mohave-Apache Community
Fort Mojave Indian Tribe (Arizona, California
and Nevada)
Gila River Indian Community
Havasupai Tribe
Hopi Tribe
Hualapai Indian Tribe
Kaibab Band of Paiute Indians
Navajo Nation (Arizona, New Mexico and
Utah)
Pascua Yaqui Tribe
Quechan Tribe (Arizona and California)
Salt River Pima-Maricopa Indian Community
San Carlos Apache Tribe
San Juan Southern Paiute Tribe

Tohono O'odham Nation
Tonto Apache Tribe
White Mountain Apache Tribe
Yavapai-Apache Nation
Yavapai-Prescott Tribe

California

Federally Recognized
Agua Caliente Band of Cahuilla Indians
Alturas Indian Rancheria
Augustine Band of Cahuilla Mission Indians
Bear River Band of the Rohnerville Rancheria
Berry Creek Rancheria of Maidu Indians of
California
Big Lagoon Rancheria
Big Pine Band of Owens Valley Paiute Shoshone
Indians
Big Sandy Rancheria of Mono Indians
Big Valley Rancheria of Pomo and Pit River
Indians
Blue Lake Rancheria
Bridgeport Paiute Indian Colony
Buena Vista Rancheria of Me-Wuk Indians
Cabazon Band of Cahuilla Mission Indians
Cachil DeHe Band of Wintun Indians of the
Colusa Indian Community
Cahuilla Band of Mission Indians
Cahto Indian Tribe
Campo Band of Diegueño Mission Indians
Capitan Grande Band of Diegueño Mission
Indians
Barona Group of Capitan Grande Band of
Mission Indians
Viejas (Baron Long) Group of Capitan Grande
Band of Mission Indians
Cedarville Rancheria
Chemehuevi Indian Tribe
Cher-Ae Heights Indian Community
Chicken Ranch Rancheria of Me-Wuk Indians
Cloverdale Rancheria of Pomo Indians
Cold Springs Rancheria of Mono Indians
Colorado River Indian Tribes (Arizona and
California)
Cortina Indian Rancheria of Wintun Indians
Coyote Valley Band of Pomo Indians

Cuyapaipe Community of Diegueño Mission
Indians
Death Valley Timbi-Sha Shoshone Band
Dry Creek Rancheria of Pomo Indians
Elem Indian Colony of Pomo Indians of the
Sulphur Bank Rancheria
Elk Valley Rancheria
Enterprise Rancheria of Maidu Indians
Fort Bidwell Indian Community
Fort Independence Indian Community of Paiute
Indians
Fort Mojave Indian Tribe (Arizona, California
and Nevada)
Greenville Rancheria of Maidu Indians
Grindstone Indian Rancheria of Wintun-Wailaki
Indians
Guidiville Rancheria
Hoopa Valley Tribe
Hopland Band of Pomo Indians
Inaja Band of Diegueño Mission Indians
Ione Band of Miwok Indians
Jackson Rancheria of Me-Wuk Indians
Jamul Indian Village
Karuk Tribe
Kashia Band of Pomo Indians of the Stewart's
Point Rancheria
La Jolla Band of Luiseño Mission Indians
La Posta Band of Diegueño Mission Indians
Los Coyotes Band of Cahuilla Mission Indians
Lytton Rancheria
Manchester Band of Pomo Indians
Manzanita Band of Diegueño Mission Indians
Mechoopda Indian Tribe
Mesa Grande Band of Diegueño Mission Indians
Middletown Rancheria of Pomo Indians
Mooretown Rancheria of Maidu Indians
Morongo Band of Cahuilla Mission Indians
Northfork Rancheria of Mono Indians
Paiute-Shoshone Indians of the Bishop
Community
Paiute-Shoshone Indians of the Lone Pine
Community
Pala Band of Luiseño Mission Indians
Paskenta Band of Nomlaki Indians
Pauma Band of Luiseño Mission Indians
Pechanga Band of Luiseño Mission Indians

Picayune Rancheria of Chukchansi Indians
Pinoleville Rancheria of Pomo Indians
Pit River Tribe (includes Big Bend, Lookout,
Montgomery Creek and Roaring Creek
Rancherias and XL Ranch)
Potter Valley Rancheria of Pomo Indians
Quartz Valley Indian Community
Quechan Tribe (Arizona and California)
Ramona Band or Village of Cahuilla Mission
Indians
Redding Rancheria
Redwood Valley Rancheria of Pomo Indians
Resighini Rancheria (formerly known as the
Coast Indian Community of Yurok Indians
of the Resighini Rancheria)
Rincon Band of Luiseño Mission Indians
Robinson Rancheria of Pomo Indians
Round Valley Indian Tribes (formerly known as
the Covelo Indian Community)
Rumsey Indian Rancheria of Wintun Indians
San Manual Band of Serrano Mission Indians
San Pasqual Band of Diegueño Mission Indians
Santa Rosa Indian Community
Santa Rosa Band of Cahuilla Mission Indians
Santa Ynez Band of Chumash Mission Indians
Santa Ysabel Band of Diegueño Mission Indians
Scotts Valley Band of Pomo Indians
Sheep Ranch Rancheria of Me-Wuk Indians
Sherwood Valley Rancheria of Pomo Indians
Shingle Springs Band of Miwok Indians
Smith River Rancheria
Soboba Band of Luiseño Mission Indians
Susanville Indian Rancheria
Sycuan Band of Diegueño Mission Indians
Table Bluff Reservation-Wiyot Tribe
Table Mountain Rancheria
Torres-Martinez Band of Cahuilla Mission
Indians
Tule River Indian Tribe
Tuolumne Band of Me-Wuk Indians
Twenty-Nine Palms Band of Luiseño Mission
Indians
United Auburn Indian Community
Upper Lake Band of Pomo Indians
Utu Utu Gwaitu Paiute Tribe

Washoe Tribe (Carson Colony, Dresslerville
Colony, Woodfords Community, Stewart
Community and Washoe Ranches)
(California and Nevada)
Yurok Tribe

Colorado

Federally Recognized
Southern Ute Indian Tribe
Ute Mountain Ute Tribe (Colorado,
New Mexico and Utah)

Connecticut

Federally Recognized
Mashantucket Pequot Tribe
Mohegan Indian Tribe

State -Recognized
Golden Hill Paugussett Tribe
Paucatuck Eastern Pequot Tribe
Schaghticoke Bands

Florida

Federally Recognized
Miccosukee Tribe of Indians
Seminole Tribe (Dania, Big Cypress, Brighton,
Hollywood and Tampa reservations)

Georgia

State-Recognized
Georgia Tribe of Eastern Cherokee
Lower Muscogee Creek Tribe
Cherokee of Georgia Tribal Council

Idaho

Federally Recognized
Coeur D'Alene Tribe
Kootenai Tribe
Nez Perce Tribe
Shoshone-Bannock Tribes

Iowa

Federally Recognized
Sac & Fox Tribe of the Mississippi

Kansas

Federally Recognized
Iowa Tribe (Kansas and Nebraska)
Kickapoo Tribe of Indians
Prairie Band of Potawatomi Indians
Sac and Fox Nation of Missouri (Kansas and
Nebraska)

Louisiana

Federally Recognized
Chitimacha Tribe
Coushatta Tribe
Jena Band of Choctaw Indians
Tunica-Biloxi Indian Tribe

State-Recognized
Caddo Indian Tribe
Choctaw-Apache of Ebarb
Clifton Choctaw
Louisiana Choctaw
United Houma Nation

Maine

Federally Recognized
Aroostook Band of Micmac Indians
Houlton Band of Maliseet Indians
Passamaquoddy Tribe
Penobscot Tribe

Massachusetts

Federally Recognized
Wampanoag Tribe of Gay Head (Aquinnah)

State-Recognized
Hassanamisco

Michigan

Federally Recognized
Bay Mills Indian Community of the Sault Ste.
    Marie Band of Chippewa Indians
Grand Traverse Band of Ottawa and Chippewa
    Indians
Hannahville Indian Community
Huron Potawatomi, Inc.
Keweenaw Bay Indian Community of L'Anse and
    Ontonagon Bands of Chippewa Indians
Lac Vieux Desert Band of Lake Superior
    Chippewa Indians
Little River Band of Ottawa Indians
Little Traverse Bay Bands of Odawa Indians
Match-she-be-nash-she-wish Band of
    Pottawatomi Indians of Michigan (Gun
    Lake Band)
Pokagon Band of Potawatomi Indians
Saginaw Chippewa Indian Tribe
Sault Ste. Marie Tribe of Chippewa Indians

State-Recognized
Burt Lake Band of Ottawa and Chippewa
    Indians
Gun Lake Band of Grand River Ottawa Indians
Swan Creek Black River Confederated Ojibwa
    Tribes
Grand River Band of Ottawa Indians

Minnesota

Federally Recognized
Lower Sioux Indian Community of Minnesota
Mdewakanton Sioux Indians
Minnesota Chippewa Tribe (Six component
    reservations: Bois Forte Band [Nett Lake],
    Fond du Lac Band, Grand Portage Band,
    Leech Lake Band, Mille Lacs Band and
    White Earth Band)
Prairie Island Indian Community of Minnesota
Mdewakanton Sioux Indians
Red Lake Band of Chippewa Indians
Shakopee Mdewakanton Sioux Community
    (Prior Lake)
Upper Sioux Indian Community

Mississippi

Federally Recognized
Mississippi Band of Choctaw Indians

Missouri

State-Recognized
Northern Cherokee
Chickamauga Cherokee

Montana

Federally Recognized
Assiniboine and Sioux Tribes
Blackfeet Tribe
Chippewa-Cree Indians
Confederated Salish and Kootenai Tribes
Crow Tribe
Fort Belknap Indian Community
Northern Cheyenne Tribe

Nebraska

Federally Recognized
Iowa Tribe (Kansas and Nebraska)
Omaha Tribe
Ponca Tribe
Sac and Fox Nation of Missouri (Kansas and
    Nebraska)
Santee Sioux Tribe
Winnebago Tribe

Nevada

Federally Recognized
Confederated Tribes of the Goshute Reservation
    (Nevada and Utah)
Duckwater Shoshone Tribe
Ely Shoshone Tribe
Fort McDermitt Paiute and Shoshone Tribes
    (Nevada and Oregon)
Fort Mojave Indian Tribe (Arizona, California
    and Nevada)
Las Vegas Tribe of Paiute Indians of the Las
    Vegas Indian Colony

Lovelock Paiute Tribe of the Lovelock Indian
    Colony
Moapa Band of Paiute Indians
Paiute-Shoshone Tribe
Pyramid Lake Paiute Tribe
Reno-Sparks Indian Colony
Shoshone-Paiute Tribes
Summit Lake Paiute Tribe
Te-Moak Tribes of Western Shoshone Indians
    (Four constituent bands: Battle Mountain,
    Elko, South Fork and Wells)
Walker River Paiute Tribe
Washoe Tribe (Nevada and California) (Carson
    Colony, Dresslerville Colony, Woodfords
    Community, Stewart Community and
    Washoe Ranches)
Winnemucca Indian Colony
Yerington Paiute Tribe
Yomba Shoshone Tribe

New Jersey

State-Recognized
Rankokus

New Mexico

Federally Recognized
Jicarilla Apache Tribe
Mescalero Apache Tribe
Navajo Nation (Arizona, New Mexico and
    Utah)
Pueblo of Acoma
Pueblo of Cochiti
Pueblo of Jemez
Pueblo of Isleta
Pueblo of Laguna
Pueblo of Nambe
Pueblo of Picuris
Pueblo of Pojoaque
Pueblo of San Felipe
Pueblo of San Juan
Pueblo of San Ildefonso
Pueblo of Sandia
Pueblo of Santa Ana
Pueblo of Santa Clara

Pueblo of Santo Domingo
Pueblo of Taos
Pueblo of Tesuque
Pueblo of Zia
Ute Mountain Tribe (Colorado, New Mexico
    and Utah)
Zuni Tribe

New York

Federally Recognized
Cayuga Nation
Oneida Nation
Onondaga Nation
Seneca Nation
St. Regis Band of Mohawk Indians
Tonawanda Band of Seneca Indians
Tuscarora Nation

State-Recognized
Poospatuck
Shinnecock

North Carolina

Federally Recognized
Eastern Band of Cherokee Indians

State-Recognized
Coharie
Haliwa-Saponi
Lumbee
Meherrin
Waccamaw-Siouan

North Dakota

Federally Recognized
Spirit Lake Tribe (formerly known as the Devil's
    Lake Sioux Tribe)
Standing Rock Sioux Tribe (North and South
    Dakota)
Three Affiliated Tribes of the Fort Berthold
    Reservation
Turtle Mountain Band of Chippewa Indians

Oklahoma

Federally Recognized
Absentee-Shawnee Tribe of Indians
Alabama-Quassarte Tribal Town
Apache Tribe
Caddo Indian Tribe
Cherokee Nation
Cheyenne-Arapaho Tribes
Chickasaw Nation
Choctaw Nation
Citizen Potawatomi Nation
Comanche Indian Tribe
Delaware Tribe of Indians
Delaware Tribe of Western Oklahoma
Eastern Shawnee Tribe
Fort Sill Apache Tribe
Iowa Tribe
Kaw Nation
Kialegee Tribal Town
Kickapoo Tribe
Kiowa Indian Tribe
Miami Tribe
Modoc Tribe
Muscogee (Creek) Nation
Osage Tribe
Ottawa Tribe
Otoe-Missouria Tribe
Pawnee Indian Tribe
Peoria Tribe
Ponca Tribe
Quapaw Tribe
Sac and Fox Nation
Seminole Nation
Seneca-Cayuga Tribe
Thlopthlocco Tribal Town
Tonkawa Tribe
United Keetoowah Band of Cherokee Indians
Wichita and Affiliated Tribes (Wichita, Keechi,
    Waco and Tawakonie)
Wyandotte Tribe

Oregon

Federally Recognized
Burns Paiute Tribe
Confederated Tribes of the Coos, Lower
    Umpqua and Siuslaw Indians
Confederated Tribes of the Grand Ronde
    Community
Confederated Tribes of the Siletz Reservation
Confederated Tribes of the Umatilla Reservation
Confederated Tribes of the Warm Springs
    Reservation Coquille Tribe
Cow Creek Band of Umpqua Indians
Fort McDermitt Paiute and Shoshone Tribes
    (Nevada and Oregon)
Klamath Indian Tribe

Rhode Island

Federally Recognized
Narragansett Indian Tribe

South Carolina

Federally Recognized
Catawba Indian Nation (Catawba Tribe)

South Dakota

Federally Recognized
Cheyenne River Sioux Tribe
Crow Creek Sioux Tribe
Lower Brule Sioux Tribe
Oglala Sioux Tribe
Rosebud Sioux Tribe
Sisseton-Wahpeton Sioux Tribe
Standing Rock Sioux Tribe (North Dakota and
    South Dakota)
Yankton Sioux Tribe

Texas

Federally Recognized
Alabama-Coushatta Tribes
Kickapoo Traditional Tribe
Ysleta Del Sur Pueblo

Utah

Federally Recognized
Confederated Tribes of the Goshute
    Reservation (Nevada and Utah)
Navajo Nation (Arizona, New Mexico and
    Utah)
Northwestern Band of Shoshoni Nation
    (Washakie)
Paiute Indian Tribe
Skull Valley Band of Goshute Indians
Ute Indian Tribe of the Uintah and Ouray
    Reservation
Ute Mountain Ute Tribe (Colorado,
    New Mexico and Utah)

Virginia

State-Recognized
Eastern Chickahominy
Chickahominy
Mattaponi
Monacan
Nansemond
Pamunkey
Rappahannock
Upper Mattaponi

Washington

Federally Recognized
Confederated Tribes of the Chehalis
    Reservation
Confederated Tribes of the Colville
    Reservation
Confederated Tribes and Bands of the Yakama
    Indian Nation
Hoh Indian Tribe
Jamestown S'Klallam Tribe
Kalispel Indian Community
Lower Elwha Tribal Community
Lummi Tribe
Makah Indian Tribe
Muckleshoot Indian Tribe
Nisqually Indian Tribe
Nooksack Indian Tribe

Port Gamble Indian Community
Puyallup Tribe
Quileute Tribe
Quinault Tribe
Samish Indian Tribe
Sauk-Suiattle Indian Tribe
Shoalwater Bay Tribe
Skokomish Indian Tribe
Snoqualmie Indian Tribe
Spokane Tribe
Squaxin Island Tribe
Stillaguamish Tribe
Suquamish Indian Tribe
Swinomish Indians
Tulalip Tribes
Upper Skagit Indian Tribe

Wisconsin

Federally Recognized
Bad River Band of the Lake Superior Tribe of
    Chippewa Indians
Forest County Potawotomi Community
Ho-Chunk Nation (formerly known as the
    Wisconsin Winnebago Tribe)
Lac Courte Oreilles Band of Lake Superior
    Chippewa Indians
Lac du Flambeau Band of Lake Superior
    Chippewa Indians
Menominee Indian Tribe
Oneida Tribe
Red Cliff Band of Lake Superior Chippewa
    Indians
Sokaogon Chippewa Community of the Mole
    Lake Band of Chippewa Indians
St. Croix Chippewa Indians
Stockbridge-Munsee Community of Mohican
    Indians

Wyoming

Federally Recognized
Arapahoe Tribe
Shoshone Tribe

REFERENCES

American Society of Legislative Clerks and Secretaries in cooperation with The National Conference of State Legislatures. *Mason's Manual of Legislative Procedure.* St. Paul, Minn.: West Publishing Company, 1989.

Berman, David R. *State and Local Politics.* Armonk, N.Y. and London, England: M.E. Sharpe Inc., 1997.

Canby, William C. *American Indian Law in a Nutshell.* St. Paul, Minn.: West Publishing Company, 1998.

Case, David S. *Alaska Natives and American Laws.* Fairbanks: University of Alaska Press, 1984.

Cohen, Felix S. *Handbook of Federal Indian Law with Reference Tables and Index.* Charlottesville, Va.: Michie Company Law Publishers, 1988.

Commission on State-Tribal Relations (former Commission of NCSL, NCAI and the National Tribal Chairman's Association). *Handbook on State-Tribal Relations.* Albuquerque, N.M.: American Indian Law Center, 1980.

Cornell, Stephen and Kalt, Joseph P. *What Can Tribes Do? Strategies and Institutions in American Indian Economic Development.* Los Angeles: American Indian Studies Center, UCLA, 1995.

Deloria, Vine Jr. *American Indian Policy in the 20ᵗʰ Century.* Norman, Okla.: University of Oklahoma Press, 1985.

Jones, Rich. " State Legislative Branch," *The Book of the States 1994-95.* Vol. 30. Lexington, Ky.: Council of State Governments, 1994.

Neal, Tommy. *A Guide to Lobby State Legislatures.* Denver, Colo.: National Conference of State Legislatures, Forthcoming.

Neal, Tommy. *Lawmaking and the Legislative Process: Committees, Connections, and Compromises.* Denver, Colo.: National Conference of State Legislatures, 1996.

O'Brien, Sharon. *American Indian Tribal Governments.* Norman, Okla.: University of Oklahoma Press, 1989.

Pevar, Stephen L. *The Rights of Indians and Tribes: The Basic ACLU Guide to Indian Tribal Rights.* Carbondale: Southern Illinois University Press, 1992.

Pound, William T. "The Modern Legislature," *State Legislatures* (July/August 1999), 28-33.

Prucha, Francis Paul. *Documents of United States Indian Policy, 2ⁿᵈ Ed. Expanded.* Lincoln, Neb. and London, England: University of Nebraska Press, 1990.

Reed, James B., and Judy Zelio, eds. *States and Tribes, Building New Traditions.* Denver, Colo.: National Conference of State Legislatures, 1995.

Tiller, Veronica. *Tiller's Guide to Indian Country, Economic Profiles of American Indian Reservation.* Albuquerque, N.M.: Bow Arrow Publishing Company, 1996.

Wilkinson, Charles F. *American Indians, Time, and the Law: Native Societies in a Modern Constitutional Democracy.* New Haven, Conn.: Yale University Press, 1988.